A Word with You America

VOLUME II

by LAWRENCE PAROS

Illustrations by DAVID MIDDLETON

A Word With You America, Volume II

Published by Kvetch Press
a division of Neurobics, Inc.
11230 75th Ave. N.E.
Kirkland, WA 98034

Illustrations by David Middleton.

Edited by Jerome M. Paros with assistance from Bandit.

ISBN: 0-9672005-1-2

Table of Contents

Economics

MONEY MATTERS

Nothing shakes up the traders of Wall street up more than a good **panic**, as it did the ancient Greeks. The Greeks, however, knew its source, the greatest trouble maker of all the pagan deities — **Pan**.

Not just your generic prankster, **Pan** struck terror into the hearts of all, from wood nymphs to human beings. Soon people began attributing to him any sudden contagious fright, naming it *panicos*, making him the source of all our **panic**.

When **panic** ensues, many **hit** or **push** the **panic button**, acting in unnecessary haste. During W.W.II, pilots aircraft bombers had a button which alerted the crew when the plane was hit and another that triggered ejection. Oft times, however, the damage was not as severe as imagined, but the pilot overreacted, pushing the button prematurely, causing the crew to bail out unnecessarily.

When all hell breaks loose, some call it **pandemonium** — from Milton's *Paradise Lost,* naming the high capital of Satan, from the Greek, *pan,* "all," and *daimon,* " spirit."

Not to fear. Prospectors once **panned** for gold, scooping small amounts of sand and gravel from streams and riverbeds. Things **panned** out when the gold settled to the bottom, and sand and gravel washed away. No thanks to the wood sprite or to Wall St., most things ultimately do **pan out** successfully.

Buy No Means

Southern Baptists threatening to stop patronizing Disney because of its policy towards Gays. So what else is new?

Back in the 19th century, Irish peasants mounted an organized campaign against the hated agent of an absentee British landlord to protest his exploitive policies. They refused to work for him, intimidated his servants, destroyed his crops, drove away his stock, and threatened his life.

In the course of being interviewed by an American journalist, the parish priest, thought "ostracism" an insufficient word to describe the approach, suggesting instead the name of the hated agent himself. The man who thus became identified forever with such a policy was Charles Cunningham **Boycott**.

Some consider a **boycott** of Disney to be nothing less than **Mickey Mouse** — "small," "petty," "inferior," "trivial," and "childish," stemming from the mid 30s when the Ingersoll watch company marketed a watch with Mickey on the face. It never kept the time properly and was always breaking down.

As to the **boycott**, it's probably less **Mickey Mouse** than just plain goofy.

In the 60s, when we "lost it," we "went ape." Nowadays, we **have a cow**.

Where would we be without them? In Anglo Saxon times, *feoh,* "cattle" and "money" were one and the the same, contributing to the **fees** we now receive. The **milch cow** (1601) gave folks a "source of regularly accruing profit," or "a person from whom money was easily drawn," helping pave the way for today's ever-dependable **cash cow**.

No one relied on cows more than the Romans who used *pecu,* "cattle," as their standard of wealth and barter, creating *pecunia,* "money," which left us **pecuniary** — whether we were into cattle futures or not. Doing well financially made us **pecunious**, not so well, **impecunious**.

Fancy this somewhat **peculiar**? **Peculiar** originally spoke of "cattle belonging solely to one person," then just "private" or "special," then "strange."

What's **peculiar** in our day and age are **sacred cows** — persons, ideas, or objects, so sacrosanct as to be exempt from criticism. In India they roam the countryside. Here you'll find them in the fields of politics, education, medicine, and law, **milking** their specialty, as we **milk** this column, for all it is worth.

The **bears and bulls** of Wall Street crashed together on October 29, 1929. Though these long standing denizens of the stock market, represent two different approaches to investment, they also share much, including a common fate.

The **bear** has his origins in an old saying, "to sell the **bearskin** before one has caught the **bear**"— defined in an 18th century dictionary as "…to sell what one hath not."

Noted for his pessimistic outlook, the **bear** sells what he hasn't yet purchased — gambling its value will drop before he has to hand it over, allowing him to turn a profit.

In truth, both the **bear** and the **bull** "hath not," it being standard practice of each to buy on the margin. The **bull** comes form the Old English *bole, bulle,* not totally unrelated to his **bollocks.** This distinguishing feature, symbolic of strength and potency, makes him **bullish** — "optimistic" and "confident." Buying low, he encourages an interest and demand in the investment , driving up its value, thus making his profit.

Not one to be confused with the Latin *bulla,* "bubble," the **bull's** speculative ventures, were also sure to burst, carrying both him and the **bear** down together.

Honey, I shrunk the **dollar**, is how the headline might have read, some seventy years ago when the Federal government reduced the size of our currency by one third — foreshadowing its declining value.

You can't say, however, that we weren't warned. **Money**, itself, derives from the Latin *moneta*, from *monere*, "to warn." **Juno Moneta** was the the Roman goddess "who gave warning" and at whose temple was established the first Roman **mint** — all of which should serve as sufficient reason to **monitor** our politicians and **admonish** them for their handling of **monetary** matters.

Mint originally was "a piece of **money**," then "**money** in general," and finally, "the place where **money** was coined." In 1518, a coin **minted** from silver from *Joachimsthal,* "Joachim's valley," was called a *Joachimsthaler*. Shortened to the *thaler*, it went on to become our **dollar**.

The almighty dollar, as an object of devotion, was coined by Washington Irving in 1836, modeled on Ben Jonson's "almighty gold," (1616).

It was George Bernard Shaw and Mark Twain, however, who thought the lack (not the love) of **money** to be the source of all evil.

A Mixed Bag

W e interrupt our regular programming in order to bring you this special bulletin: "Congress **bags budget,** people left holding **bag**."

"What is our representatives' bag?" you ask. When cockfights were in vogue, owners used to bring their birds to the pits in a sack. Asked their chance of victory, they'd confidently remark, **"It's in the bag**," a term we use today as a general expression of assurance.

The Romans confidently kept their coins in a small, leather bag called a *bulga*, creating the **bulge** in our pockets. It also gave us the Old French *bougette* or "wallet/bag," making for our **budget** — a bag now **bulging** to the breaking point and demanding our attention.

Byrsa is Greek for the leather of which the bag was made. This gave us our **bursar**, "a financial officer of a college or university," as well as our **purse**.

When you next **purse** your lips, think of it as a small bag, closed by pulling a thong — the same as when you **pucker** up, from the French, *faire des poches*, "to make little bags."

You'll find it especially appropriate when reading about the trillion dollar Federal **budget**. It'll help you understand that when it comes to government spending, you can truly kiss your dollars goodbye.

Whatever happened to balancing the budget? After years of warnings and admonitions, we've finally become thoroughly acclimated to critics pointing out the evils of **deficit** spending, from the Latin *deficere*, "to be wanting" or "to lack" — pointing up a serious **defect** in the system and a **deficiency** in executive and legislative leadership.

And now...there's talk of a surplus. Shades of Ross Perot!

Could there really be an end in sight? Literally, yes — **finance**, once having been a payment that settled accounts and brought matters quickly to a conclusion.

It also related to both payment of a penalty that resolved matters, a "**fine**," and an adjective describing the good and **final** feeling accompanying closure.

The Latin *finis*, a "settled payment," is at the root of all these words. How fitting that it also came to spell the end of things!

Before becoming too self-congratulatory, perhaps Congress and the President both need be reminded of the value of the **finite** and the **finished** product; i.e. learn to **confine** discussions, and **define** the issues better before writing **finis** to such matters.

Only then may we say, "How **fine** it is!"

CHAPTER 2

Making it
UP, UP, AND AWAY

Waiting for your ship to come in?
It's a concept that first took hold during the 19th century as merchants anxiously anticipated the return of ships, carrying their valuable cargo from distant places.

So too do many of us wait for new-found prosperity to come our way. It may be a while however. Many find their ship **at sea** — "adrift, and without direction."

Could you have **lost your bearings**? When you **take your bearings**, you determine your relative position by employing celestial or geographic references.

Not all is lost. There's always the intervention of *Portunus*, the Roman protecting god of harbors. It's he who ensures that landings happen in a timely, appropriate, or **opportune** fashion, from the Latin, *op-, ob-,* "towards," and *portus*, "harbor." The occasion of your ship's arrival is a moment filled with promise, making it everything an **opportunity** could be.

Tired of waiting? Rather than just trusting in the Gods, you can always take the helm and create your own **opportunities**. All you have to do is adapt to existing conditions by **trimming your sails** — simply "accommodating them to the way the winds are blowing."

We all love our jobs, but each of us looks at the **pay-off** in a different way. .

Some think in terms of promises made — **wages** originally being "pledges"or "declarations to **pay**." Others consider it primarily a form of pacification — **pay** deriving from the French *payer,* from the Latin *pacer,* "to appease," from *pax- pac-,* "peace."

Many simply grind it out each day, receiving **emoluments** for their efforts, from the Latin *emolere,* "to grind," the profits once having come primarily from milling.

The more "esteemed" members of the workforce, however, would never deign to receive anything less than a high **salary**, which they proceed to salt away as fast as they can.

Roman soldiers were once paid in salt, a precious commodity, used both for seasoning and as a preservative. Though money for its purchase was later substituted for the salt itself, it remained *salarium* or "salt money," creating our first **salaries**.

The salt of the earth were noted in Matt. 5:13, where Jesus encourages the poor in spirit, the merciful, those persecuted for the sake of righteousness, the peacemakers, and the pure of heart, " Ye are **the salt of the earth**...the light of the world." Leaving us to wonder as to who today is **worth their salt**?

THE WRONG SIDE...

It's a killer job. A career move. To make a good impression, you put your **best foot forward.** First day on the job and you're trying to **get off on the right foot.**

When the Romans **put their best foot forward,** it was always the right one. Tradition required they always enter or leave a room or dwelling by first stepping off **on the right foot.**

Getting off on the right foot once meant rising properly in the morning so that your right foot hit the floor first. Failure to do so could spell ill-fortune.

History records how Augustus Caesar attributed a major defeat on the battlefield to having hastily placed his left-footed sandal on before his right, the morning prior to battle.

Grouchy and ill disposed after only a month on the job? Knowing you had hit the floor with the wrong foot first that morning could only make you feel moody and ill-tempered the rest of the day — leaving others wondering what was afoot.

Little did they know that you simply had gotten out on **the wrong side of the bed**.

Getting the Boot

How to make it to the top in America? All it takes is a little grit. Anyone can do it. The directions are simple. Just **pull yourself up by your own bootstraps**.

By the little loop sewn to the side of the boot? You gotta be kidding! Pulling on the loop may enable you to more easily get the boot on, but you can't pull yourself up in this manner, though we've encouraged people to do so since the late 19th century.

Perhaps they needed some inspiration. **A Horatio Alger Story** perchance — one featuring intrepid souls, such as Rugged Dick, who through hard work and clean living, overcame insurmountable odds to achieve success.

Alas, though Alger's heroes bettered themselves — some even gaining fame and glory — few ever hit it big financially. His fiction was dull and preachy. His real life story was scandalous — a young minister charged with "the abominable and revolting crime of unnatural familiarity with boys" who when confronted with the charges, left town.

Alger resettled in New York City where his work with boys at the Newsboys Lodging House provided him with material for the books that went on to become synonymous with the National Dream. Only in America.

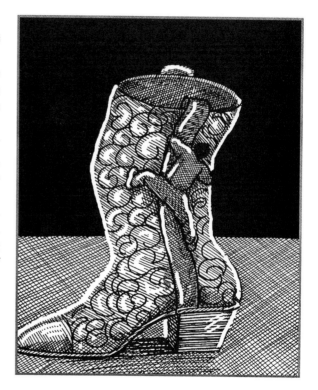

Round and round it goes and where it stops, nobody knows. The wheel finally stopped turning in 1970, on the TV version of "The Original Amateur Hour" — one of the longest running shows for entertainers seeking their shot at **fame** and **fortune**.

The **Fame** they sought was having the "right" people talking about them. According to Romans, it wasmafter the Gods had spoken, from *fari, fatum*, "to speak," that your **fate** was sealed, — *fama* being the talk that shaped your future and gave you **fame**.

Before 1200, **fame** conveyed "good character."Only later, did it connote "general renown." When the Gods spoke highly of you, it made you **famous**; badly, **infamous**. There's really not much to it. What people are **famous** or **infamous** for is being **famous** or **infamous**.

Life being not unlike TV, it's all short lived. *Sic transit gloria.* Not to fear however. We have at least the fifteen minutes promised to us by Andy Warhol back in 1968.

This includes "**The rich and the famous**," a TV series celebrating their lives, the phrase popularized earlier by Truman Capote in his "Breakfast at Tiffany's" in 1961.

As to their wealth, there's not much to talk about, *fors,* "chance" or "luck,"explaining how many made their **fortunes**.

Who knows when **the fickle finger of fate** may beckon you to stardom? So began the popular segment of Rowan and Martin's "Laugh-In" (1968-73) — offering that award to the winner of a mock talent contest.

Fingering also has its negative side. Who of us hasn't suffered the ignominy of being **f****d by the fickle finger of fate** (1940s) — a favorite expression of the Canadian Armed forces for an unpredictable and particularly injurious event?

It was Shakespeare who first **pointed the finger at another** in *Othello* — "To make me the fixed figure for the time of Scorne to point his slow, and moving finger at." Though blame has been **at our fingertips** only since the second half of the19th century.

Helping further asseess blame, were **fingerprints,** first put into use by law enforcement agencies on October 10, 1904, assisting us in **fingering** the guilty party.

None of this is to be confused with **giving the finger to someone**, the meaning of which is universal — though from 1890-1920, it meant simply "to disappoint or snub someone."

A popular expression of discontent on our nation's highways, the gesture goes back to Ancient Rome where charioteers passed each other while offering the ***digitus impudicus***.

To make it in today's changing world, you've got to learn to **go with the flow**.

What better way than with the the Latin *fluere*? Start each workday starts with your morning latte, followed by your hourly swig of Evian — replenishing your precious bodily **fluids**.

Your **fluency** in the new computer program astounds your colleagues, as your **mellifluous** presentations flow effortlessly, like honey, (*mel, mellis*) "smooth" and "sweet," from your mouth.

Coupled with your ability to avoid **superfluous** asides, literally an "overflow of information," you begin to exercise some **influence** — a term used in astrology for forces determined by the "flowing" of the stars. This leads to a prestigious position and a more **affluent** lifestyle, where good things simply "flow towards" you.

You're now riding the wave of success.

In the business world, however, things are always in **flux**. Management writes it off as a trickle, but there is an increasing **influx** of new talent into the organization. Your good fortune **fluctuates**, "rising and falling like the waves." This leads to the Old French *flus,* "flow." Once **flushed** with pride, you watch helplessly as a promising career is **flushed** away.

There's no stemming the tide. It's a wipeout.

Looking to knock 'em dead at work with your new attire? Start beneath the surface with your **boxers**, similar to those worn by a combatant entering a ring. Outside, your **khakis** from the Sepoy rebellion in India and a **blazer f**rom Britain's *H.M.S. Blazer* — a 19th century British Man-of-War on which the Captain ordered his men to wear blue and white striped jerseys.

Tying it all together, a matching **cravat** from the French, *cravate,* for a "Croatian," referring to the mercenaries in the Thirty Years War (1618-48), noted for the huge colorful scarf knotted loosely round their neck.

Your **cardigan's** courtesy of James Thomas Brudenell, Seventh *Earl of Cardigan,* the overbearing British General who led the charge of the Light Brigade in the Crimean War .

No better way to kick the competition's rear than with your new **bluchers** from Prussian Field Marshal *Gebhard Leberecht Von Blücher* who after decking out all his men in this low-laced footwear, gave the boot to Napoleon at Waterloo.

What better way to top it all off than with a **trench coat** worn by British officers during W.W.I and an attaché case gripped tightly in your hand?

Consider yourself now dressed to kill.

Present Arms!

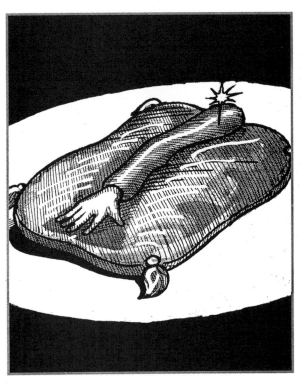

The secret of success in business today is having a good **right hand** man at your side. If you don't believe it, look at the historical record.

Ancient Greek seers during augury faced North, with the East, the lucky side on their right, and West, the unlucky on their left.

Judas sat *ad sinistram*, at Christ's left at the Last Supper; while the "good thief" who was crucified, sat at Christ's right.

Christ, himself, was said to have sat at God's right-hand side and those depicted so in relation to him were always deemed to be the most virtuous, making for the concept of the **right-hand man**.

You can always count on your **right hand man**. He's the epitome of trust and loyalty.

On the battlefield he occupied a key position of responsibility and command to the right of the troop of horse guards. He was also the confidante and bodyguard who stood by his master's right, the better to draw his sword in a moment of need with his strong hand — the right, of course.

Nowadays your **right hand** man is often a former Girl-Friday. The ultimate sacrifice he or she could make? **Give his (or her) right arm** for you — what else?

There's the Rub

Asserting your authority by **riding roughshod** over your subordinates?

It's one way to advance, but not without cost. The **roughshod** horse has the nails on its shoes projecting outward. Though the technique affords more sure-footed progress, it also damages the ground being traveled.

Riding roughshod at the office, you treat others abusively — acting with total disregard for their feelings, advancing ruthlessly at their expense.

Perhaps you're just **chagrined,** because something was rubbing you the wrong way. Historically, it was the Turkish *saghri,* the "harsh leather" of your saddle or another part of your riding equipment that irritated your behind. Today, it's more likely that rump of a boss getting under your skin.

Best you just stand tall in the saddle. Take heart in the original meaning of **chagrin,** and how in the end you'll emerge all the tougher for it.

Above all, let up a bit. If you want to **win** the respect of your associates **hands down,** try acting like a jockey, who certain of victory, drops his hands, thus loosening his hold on the reins.

You'll then be home free "with a hearty hi-yo Silver! Away!"

Stomach in knots? You're probably **strung out**, from the Latin, *stringere, strict-,* to "draw tight," "contract," or "bind" — its past participle *strictus,* creating the **strict** demands you make on yourself and the **stress** in your life.

Stress is necessary. The problem is **distress** — "being pulled apart" or "torn asunder," from *dis-,* "away" and *stringere,* "to stretch." You'll simply have to learn how to **restrain** yourself — from *restringere,* to "bind back" or "hold in check."

What's put you in such a bind? Adding *prae,* "before" to *stingere,* gave you *praestringere,* "to bind before." Binding something before your eyes ends up blindfolding you.

So too with *praestigiae,* originally a "conjurer's trick." Dazzling and charming the spectators, it made for **prestige,** the illusive goal for which you have been **straining**.

Think of it as sleight of hand. Joining the Latin *prestus,* "ready" or "quick" to *digitator,* "manipulator," from *digitus,* "finger," created the **prestidigitator** who makes things disappear with his fingers.

Prestige. Presto chango! — now you see it, now you don't.

The successful person today is on the go. Your **career** demands nothing less — deriving as it does from the French, *carrière* from the Latin *car,* "chariot," from *currere, curs-,* "to run."

Initially, a **career** described a "road" or "race track," then the running of it at full speed.

Today's **career** is also filled with movement. The race, as we all know, goes to the swift.

Propelling you towards the finish line is your personal **ambition,** from the Latin *amb,* "about" and *ire,* "to go," creating *ambitio,* "a going about or around" — referring to Roman political candidates, pounding the pavement for votes.

Ambition today has broadened to include any passion for honor and power. **Ambitious** people still get around, but they're not doing much **ambling.** As the subject of a driving **ambition,** they're more likely behind the wheel of a BMW.

The grand prix for today's **careerists** is the **rat race** (mid 20thC.), from the image of laboratory rats on a treadmill, desperately and fiercely competing to maintain or improve their position.

Winner takes all. But as one wag noted, "The winner of a **rat race** is still a rat."

Who exactly is in charge here?

During the 19th century, they asked "**who's rolling the big wheel?**" — making for both our **big wheel** (c.1950) and our **wheeler dealer** (mid 1950's) — two guys who have been on a roll ever since.

The one over there with all the appeal, he's the **top banana**. As the lead comedian in burlesque, he often wielded a soft, water or air-filled banana-shaped club with which he hit lesser ranked comedians on the head.

He's also the **honcho,** from *han,* "squad" and *cho,* "leader." a term U.S. soldiers picked up while stationed in Japan during the post-war occupation.

Also making the transition to civilian life was the **V.I.P.**, your "very important person," first introduced during W.W.II by an Air Force officer trying to keep secret the names of the important personages on a secret flight to the Mid-East.

Fame, however, is fleeting. Not every **big wheel**, **top banana**, **honcho**, or **V.I.P**. endures the test of time.

Witness **the big bug** (c.1827) — quashed in his tracks, before he could even make it into the 20th century.

When words fail to describe the new CEO, simply smile and say **cheese,** as in **the big cheese**.

Frenchmen also know him as **le grand fromage**.

Closer scrutiny, however, shows the dairy industry is in no way associated with your boss or with any other powerful personage.

First recorded in America in 1914, he had assumed prominence earlier in mid-19th century England as "**the cheese,**" for "the thing," "the correct thing," or the "best" — a little something the British picked up in India from the Urdu *chiz* or *cheez* for "thing."

Shocked by it all? Feel free to register surprise, disbelief, or disappointment by screaming "**Cheese!**" It's only a compressed and corrupted version of *Jesus*!

"**Cheese it!**" you say. That's simply "cease it!" — the staple of gangster films of the 20's and 30's as in "**Cheese it, the cops!**"

Big Cheese throwing a reception? A little brie and chablis. What else?

You can always count on high **muck-a-mucks** to throw a good feed — as did the Chinook Indians with their *hiu muckamuck*, "plenty of food." Now about that **big enchilada**...

Netscape vs. Microsoft — the joy of victory, the **agony** of defeat. The Greek *agein*, "to lead, "gave us *agon* — an "assembly," into which people were led to witness the public games.

Once comfortably seated, you watched the *Agonia,* "the contest or struggle for the prize" and your favorite *agonistes,* "contender" — creating our first **antagonists,** those you rooted *anti,* "against" and the **protagonists**, those you rooted *pro*, "for."

Eventually, *agonia* came to describe not the struggle but the mental and physical anguish experienced in its course.

Agony then extended to "any activity fraught with difficulty or pain;" later, "anguish" and "intolerable pain," before arriving at its current definition" — "any extreme suffering of body or mind ."

For sheer **agony** you went to Rome for gladiatorial contests — extremely violent events held in amphitheaters, the floor of which were covered with sand to lend stable footing and absorb the blood of the combatants.

Over time, the sand and the fighting area became linked — making *harena*, Latin for "sand," into the **arena** — the field of play or the actual building or stadium where sporting events are held. No accident that the corporate **arena** is now the area of greatest contemporary bloodletting.

CHAPTER 3

Consumerism

THE SWEET BUY AND BUY

For a product to be successful, it must have **brand** recognition. Originally, a **brand** was simply "a piece of burning wood" or "a torch," then "a blade of a sword," alluding to its glint. About 1552, it took on the meaning of "ownership," validated by burning an item with a hot iron. Then in 1827, a "trademark" and in 1854, a "particular sort of goods indicated by a trademark." Thus would **brand** names be etched indelibly in our memory.

That a product is **brand new** (c.1570) also helps — like metals or metal articles which shine as if fresh from the forge. It's a term synonymous with **fire-new** — a phrase used several times by Shakespeare.

What also helps is a good catch phrase. A *slogorne* was the battle cry used by Scottish Highland clans, borrowed from the Gaels *sluagh-ghairm,* from *slaugh,* "army" and *gairm,* "shout." This helped us to shout out our first **slogan** in 1680, which then went on to become "a distinctive word or phrase used by a particular group" in 1704.

Brandishing their **brand new** weapons, Madison Ave. sounds the cry for yet another assault on the minds and hearts of the American people.

If you find store clerks rude and discourteous, it's because the relationship between the purchaser and the vendor is no longer what it used to be.

Since the 15th century we've known the purchaser primarily as a **customer**. It's a good word — the *custom* in **customer** implying something of a regular and continuing relationship between the seller and the buyer.

In recent times, however, the **customer** has been replaced by the **consumer**. And the role of the **consumer** is to simply use up what is produced — in short, to **consume.**

Consume's roots can be found in the Latin *consumere*, "to take up completely," "devour," or "spend." The word has never conveyed anything of a positive nature — only destruction, waste, and exhaustion. Lovers are **consumed** by unbridled passion, as the illness called **consumption** sweeps through their ravaged bodies.

Feeling thoroughly spent from all that shopping? Your credit record is one of your most prized possessions. Go for broke! FOB. COD. SOB. SOS. IOU. Right on the dotted line.

Just keep on **consuming**! It's now the custom.

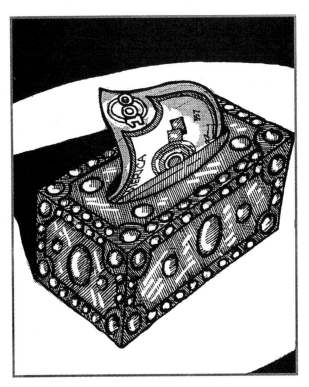

*C*redit cards maxed out? There are alternatives.

In simpler times, merchants kept perishable items in barrels to retain their freshness. After selecting the item you wanted to purchase from the barrel, you conveniently left your money atop the container — making **cash on the barrelhead** synonymous with "cash on the spot."

For those not so disposed, storekeepers and bartenders took IOUs, recording debts on their shirt cuffs. Cuffs were then made of celluloid allowing creditors to write on them in pencil and later wipe them clean. They were also portable and, like the collars, were not sewn to the shirt. **Putting it on the cuff** made for convenient bookkeeping — though the added interest caused many to later lose their shirt.

Nothing new here. Usury and extortion have long been a part of Western history. During the 9th century, the Danes imposed a special tax on the Irish whose lands they occupied. Those who refused to pay were punished by having their nose slit.

Nothing to be sneezed at, we've all been **paying through the nose** ever since.

It's the moment of truth—time to own up to your great holiday shopping binge. A time to sort bills and stare blankly at your checkbook, **tallying** the damage, thanks to the Old French *tallier*, "to cut" and its derivation from the Low Latin *taliare*, from *talis*, "like," in reference to two equal parts.

Tallying derives from a long-standing system of taking a stick, marking it on each end with notches indicating the number or quantity of goods delivered, and then cutting it in half so that each of the two principals had the same record. As a check, the seller kept one half, the purchaser the other. It's not unlike the merchant's and the customer's copy of today's charge.

Those kept from Norman times by the Royal Exchequer were as long as six feet. The officials who kept the sticks were called *telliers* who later found a place in the banking system as **tellers.**

The pressure you feel while **tallying** up the damage are a form of **retaliation** from the merchant for the demands you have made on him—from the Latin *re*, "back" + *talis*, "like." This appropriate response comes from the **retailer** who originally dealt in such small items that he could keep his records by **tally.** Anyway you cut it, it's sure to stick.

Chances are that during the holiday season you spent a bit too **lavishly** — from the Old French *lavasse*, a deluge of rain, from the Latin *lavare*, "to wash," Money apparently went through your hands like water.

Après le deluge, the flood of bills, comes a time for assessment. Perhaps you were in a daze at the time, causing you to go beyond the bounds of reason and spend **extravagantly**. After all, the word does come from the Latin *extra* "on the outside" and *vagus, vagans,* "wandering."

Did all that wandering cause you to finally **buy it**? The British first introduced the notion that when you **buy it**, you die. First used in the military early in the 19th century, **buying it** soon became a witty way of saying that you had paid for an action with your life.

As we prepared to **buy it,** the last words to pass our lips were "Slap it on the plastic!"

The Greek *plassein* from which we get our **plastic** literally "molds"and "shapes" our post-holiday activity.

But like the substance itself, ever so flexible and easy to work with in its early stages, once it has set and hardened, what you see is what you get.

In the hole financially?

It's never easy getting out of any hole. But it became even trickier during the early 1900s when gambling establishments cut a slot in the middle of the table leading to a locked compartment below. Into that hole went a certain percentage of money wagered that belonged to the house, as well as I.O.U.'s, and large bills. Everything that went **down that hole** represented house profits and players' lossses.

How to get **out of the hole**? A rope might help. It could also lead to new entanglements. **Liabilities** have a way of doing that — from the Latin, *ligare*, "to tie or restrain," like all those things in your life that hold you back.

There's your job that makes you feel like a serf — making your boss into a **liege** to whom you're bound in service. Attractive new job offers test your **allegiance,** or ties to him. Why the very thought of it makes the old bod ache all over, every **ligament** in your body screaming out for help. A-i-e-e-e! It's beginning to feel like all your woes are in **league** with one another.

Time perhaps to loosen up. You might start by counting your **assets.** The Latin *ad satis* should leave you "sated" or "satisfied"— putting your frustrations to rest as well as your debts.

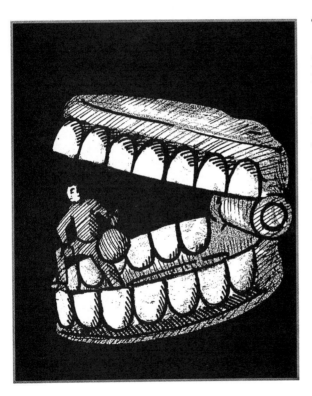

The latest estimate is that thirty eight percent of our income goes towards taxes. If true, it's a pretty significant bite out of your paycheck. It's enough to make you feel like a slave or, at worst, an **indentured servant**.

You do remember **indentured servants** from junior high — those good people who traded years of future work for passage to the New World? The agreement they entered into was a contract with real teeth in it. After signing, the **articles of indenture**, from the Latin, *in*, "in" and *dens,* "tooth," the paper was torn in half, leaving toothed or jagged edges in each, making it possible to later check the genuineness of either half by matching them up.

It also allowed us to **indent**.

Indenture aside, **taxes** make a real **dent** in our bank account. We once paid **taxes** by doing some predetermined work, the completion of certain **tasks**, being our first **taxes.**

Going to the **dentist** and paying **taxes** are **tasks**, both of which are akin to pulling teeth. Is there anything you can do about it? Shakespeare suggested to York in Henry VI , that he "sit and fret and **bite his tongue**" — "suffer in silence" — leaving us with very little in which to sink our teeth. .

CHAPTER 4

Food

WHAT'S COOKIN'

Some of us marvel at the ease with which President Clinton moves from crisis to crisis.

What appears initially a monumental challenge, turns out to be " **a piece of cake**" — from an R.A.F. expression of the late 1930s for an "easy task" — like swallowing a delicious dessert item.

It's also a **cake walk**, from a simple and enjoyable walk around dance competition initiated by slaves in the early 1800s — featuring high stepping, high kicking couples. The top couple received a prize for their stylistic strut, as the President was rewarded for his nimble dancing about the charges.

"**That takes the cake**," you say. Indeed. That *was* the prize, a custom dating back to Ancient times. We're somewhat ambivalent about it today, using the phrase to characterize something either outrageously good or bad.

How does it all go down with the public? *"Qu'ils mangent de la brioche"* "**Let them eat cake**." Columnist Westbrook Pegler noted that what Marie Antoinette should have said was, "Let them eat hokum." Unfortunately, she never even made the original remark. Worse yet, a *brioche* is more like a bun or a scone.

When it comes to politicians, better they should eat their words, and just pass on the napoleons.

Big Macs in Moscow, Berlin, Tokyo! Who won the war anyway? Let's kick our former enemies' buns, not fill 'em with cheese, onions, and pickles.

Let's begin by getting a few facts straight. An all-American item, the **burger** originated not in **Hamburg** Germany, but in **Hamburg, New York** where one day in the summer of 1885 Charles and Frank Menches, vendors at the Erie county fair, ran short of meat and saved the day by falling back on their creation. Though a **hamburger steak** had been sighted on Delmonico's menu fifty years earlier.

No matter. What really got **hamburgs** on a roll was putting them on a roll. Sites from Connecticut to Kentucky lay claim to first having done the deed. But it was the White Castle chain that really put it on the map — a nickel getting you a one ounce **White Castle** on a bun.

They were soon joined by **Wimpeyburgers,** from the Popeye cartoon character who downed prodigious amounts, and finally the **Big Mac** and the **Whopper**.

Don't forget. We may have sold our birthright for a mess of rubles, yen, and rupees, but when it comes to junk food, we are **the mustard** (19th C.) — "the genuine article or main attraction."

A frank discussion. The item under consideration was introduced into the United States by an immigrant from **Frankfurt** named Antoine Feuchtwanger. It then surfaced into the language during the 1920s as a **tube steak**. and a **wienerwurst** — a "Vienna sausage," later shortened to a **wiener.**

Harry Stevens, the concessionaire, was the first to serve it as a grilled **frank** on a split roll about 1901, ordering his vendors at the old Polo Grounds to yell, "Get your **red-hots!**" H.L .Mencken, was somewhat less enthusiastic about the delicacy, calling it "a cartridge filled with the sweepings of abattoirs."

But it was the prolific word inventor and sports cartoonist, T.A. Dorgan, who labeled it a **hot dog** — casting aspersions as to its main ingredient by drawing a dachshund on a roll. This designation was not well received by the Coney Island Chamber of Commerce who proceeded to ban the use of the term.

The **hot dog**, however, never took it lying down. Around 1906, "**Hot dog!**" became an ejaculation of approval, delight and gratification. It also came to characterize one who performed in a brilliant or spectacular manner, and loved playing to the audience. Someone we could truly relish.

It began with John Montagu, the Fourth Earl of **Sandwich** (1718-92) and British First Lord of the Admiralty whose name first designated the islands now known as Hawaii. We remember him best though as the inveterate gambler who improvised a meal at the card tables.

It took the Americans, however, to make the **sandwich** what it is today. The **Western** was a creation of our pioneers, consisting of foodstuffs mashed up with eggs to disguise the foul odor caused by lack of refrigeration.

The **club sandwich** originated in the 1920s, a favorite of the country club set — the only ones who could afford the ingredients.

Others were left with the **poor boy,** sighted first in New Orleans in the late 19th century, a complete meal unto itself. — vegetables, meat, cheeses, et al. Because the poor were its initial recipients, they came to name it as well.

The **Italian hero sandwich** was decorated in New York about 1920, later reduced to a **hero** and ultimately **submarine**d, **torpedo**ed, and **rocket**ed to prominence regionally, where it was reduced in rank to a **hoagie** and a **grinder**. How soon they forget.

An order of **fries** to go. Thanks to Thomas Jefferson. A long time advocate of the potato, our third President was the first to legitimize it as food. It didn't stop there however. During his ambassadorship to France, he became enamored with a side dish that originated with Belgium peasants in the 17th century. It was called *pommes frites*, (**french**) **fried potatoes** — **frenching** being synonymous with "cutting into slivers or thin strips."

On returning home, he introduced them to his countrymen at Monticello. During the 1870s, they were considered a delicacy, within thirty years, a common dish. As their popularity increased, they were shortened to **french frieds** in the 1920s, **french fries** in the 30s, and plain old **fries** in the 60s.

To the British, they've always been **chips**, as in **fish and chips**. We joined them in the 1870s when a chef at a spa at Saratoga Springs, New York created a hit with his paper-thin fried potatoes, and Americans everywhere started **chipping** away.

Chips are the staple of **the couch potato** — all eyes and round body, born on July 15, 1976, trademarked by a Tom Iacino of Pasadena California for his organization. **The couch potato** first surfaced in Pasadena's Doo Dah Parade in '79, gained currency from '85-'96, and has been in active repose ever since.

What's in a name? A lot if it's **Coca Cola.** Ask the student in a Georgia high school who was suspended for wearing a Pepsi T-shirt on a day on which **Coke** was being honored.

The poor lad clearly knew nothing of its illustrious history.

Dr. John B. Pemberton, a 19th century Atlanta pharmacist, created the drink, brewing the syrup in a kettle in his backyard. He later chased the syrup with carbonated water, bottled it, and marketed it as a delicious "French Wine Coca-Ideal Nerve and Tonic Stimulant." The concoction proved not only refreshing but a fine picker-upper as well — thanks to the cocaine he added..

Though most of the cocaine was replaced by caffeine in 1886, its name was changed to **Coca-Cola** — referring to the coca leaf and the cola nut. Embarrassed by the cocaine reference, new ownership later tried to suppress the name. Unable to do so, they reluctantly registered it as a trademark. Things changed, however, as the popularity of the drink and its name soared. They then went to court more than 7,000 times to fully retain its exclusive use. Ironically, during the 1960s it came full circle as an abbreviated street version of cocaine.

Hopefully, this information will be eventually be integrated into our schools' curricula. Grades, after all, do go better with...

A delicacy for more than 3,000 years it began life as flavored snow or ice, and was a favorite of such notables as Marco Polo, Montezuma II, and George Washington.

Its fans were always enthusiastic. During the gay nineties, children called out, **"Hokey Pokey, a penny a lump, the more you eat the more you jump."** More recently, **"I scream, you scream, we all scream for ice cream!"**

They really jumped for joy in the early 1890s when the owner of a Wisconsin ice cream parlor created a special only-on-Sunday ice cream treat, appropriately dubbed a **Sunday**. Verbal affect later transformed it into our **sundae**.

For the inside scoop, however, we look to September 22, 1903 when Italo Marchiony, pushcart entrepreneur extraordinaire of New York City, filed an application for a patent.

Three months later US Patent No. 746971 was issued for a mold, initially made of paper, later of pastry, to hold the ices he dispensed.

It went on to become a popular favorite at the St. Louis World's fair of 1904 where the ice cream vendor and the nearby pastry man creatively joined forces. By 1909, **the ice cream cone** was on the tongue of all America. All in "good humor" of course.

Have you had your **veggies** recently? Don't knock 'em. Closer examination shows their roots are truly exciting, going back to the Medieval Latin *vegetabilis*, "growing or flourishing," from *vegetare*, "to grow or enliven," which in turn derives from *vegere*, *vegetus*, "to arouse" or "impart vigor." A close kin to *vigere*, "to flourish," they're what make us both **vigorous** and **vigilant**.

Vegetables came to fruition in America in 1935 when "Popeye the Sailorman," the cartoon creation of E.C. Segar, first appeared on the radio. We would never again look at **spinach** the same way. Some think it derives from the Latin *spina*, "thorn," referring to its appearance. If you're wondering where Popeye got his backbone, look no further.

Thanks to **spinach**, he was no match for either the **spineless** Brutus or the nation's poor nutritious habits. During the 1930s, **spinach** growers in the United States credited him for a 33% increase in the consumption of the vegetable. In honor of his achievement, he became the first cartoon character to be immortalized in a public sculpture, in Crystal City, Texas.

Alas, Popeye is now the number one licensed character food brand in the world, promoting fried chicken, frozen foods, and Pepsi. Better he should have just **vegetated**.

Another weekend dining out, indulging yourself, eating **high off the hog** (late19thC).

Why not? That's where you'll traditionally find the choicest cuts of meat — high up on the hog's side.

You say you **ate like a bird,** thinking birds don't eat very much. In truth, relative to their size, they eat considerably.

The moment of truth comes when you step on the bathroom scale. Your bravado crumbles, and a sumptuous breakfast gives way to **eating humble pie** (early 19thC). You are absolutely mortified. The *umbles* were the heart, liver, and entrails of the deer, a little something left for the servants while the Lord and Lady feasted on the venison. Having to eat the *umbles* suggested poverty, a **humble** status, and your current humiliation. The only thing you can now swallow is your pride.

The call to a hearty breakfast, however, still beckons. "But a **morsel**," you say, from the Latin *mors* , a "bite," from *mordere*, "to bite."

You hesitate for a moment. Adding *re,* "back," leads to a "biting again and again," "vexing" you, creating a sense of **remorse** (1385) — a gnawing feeling that can only leave you **eating your words** (1550s).

CHAPTER 5

Sports

FAIR GAME

The Naked truth about organized sports. Read all about it!

The Ancient Greek physician, Hippocrates claimed the sun had healthful and curative powers that strengthened the body.

There being no better way to receive these benefits than going au naturel, Greek boys and men often performed collective exercises, including the Olympics, in the nude.

Gymnos is Greek for "naked," and *gymnazo*, "to train naked." That training ultimately evolved into our **gymnastics** — an activity most frequently performed today in the confines of a **gymnasium** by **gymnasts** somewhat clothed.

Ancient Greece was also where organized sports first shed its innocence with the introduction of extrinsic rewards. It was there that contestants first vied in competition for a winning prize called the *athlon*.

As the prize and its pursuit became the primary objective, it became more closely associated with those contesting for it. Ultimately, it named them — creating our modern-day **athletes**.

It also shaped their character and motivation, described by many as "naked greed."

When it comes to organized sports, we, the spectators, have a lot to **contend** with. Not only do we have to deal with the **contending** teams but also the **bones of contention** between the owners and the players.

Things were much simpler during the 16th century when **casting a bone of contention** first stretched itself metaphorically beyond the discord caused by throwing a group of dogs a bone.

At the root of our contemporary discord is the Latin *tendere,* "to stretch." and *contendere* asking athletes to " stretch themselves <u>with</u> all their strength." There's also a **tendon** in there to be stretched, but only if you have the **intention** of doing so.

It's easy to **pretend** that sports are still played for the love of the game. That however, would be "stretching things a bit <u>before</u> (the fact)." It also ignores the **tension** between labor and management which threatens to tear the game apart.

What it **portends** is that we "stretch or look <u>forward,</u>" to a day when both players and owners see the important issues to which they must **attend** and **extend,** "stretch or reach <u>out</u>" their hands to each other and to those who follow them.

49

The amateur command little respect. His name is synonymous with the clumsy beginner, the inexperienced and the unskilled. Things **amateurish** are considered second rate and unworthy of our attention.

Some are even considered **hams**, "those who overact and exaggerate" — from the cockney *hamateur*, as a word-play on its original roots. These **hams**, however, more likely come from the designation for the thigh and buttocks, an appropriate body location with which such a performer might be identified — helping make for the doltish and clumsy *ham-fat man* or *hamfatter* of the early minstrel shows. Though one could also argue for the hamfat or lard he used to remove his stage makeup.

If you're looking for the real **hams,** look not to the NCAA tournament, but to professional sports. It's there the **hams** and hot dogs abound. Hats off to the college kids who reminded us how sports were played before the era of agents and multi-million dollar contracts, those who play not for money but for the love of the game. They are **amateurs**, in the purest sense of the word — from the Latin *amare, amat-,* "to love." And they play the game with all their heart.

No one does it quite like the **professional**. The **professional**, or **pro**, as we like to call him, comes from the Latin *professus,* "declaring," which made for the Middle English, *professed,* "declared for God," or "bound by religious vows." Seemingly, we vest in our **professions** all the trappings of a religious order, treating them as closed and highly coveted circles.

Sports is one area where the **professional** rules supreme. The first **professional** baseball team was the Cincinnati Redstockings of 1869, marking the first time players were openly paid a salary. The brother of the manager, the shortstop, was the highest paid at $1,400 for the season. The team finished the season with a 65-0 record and a profit of $1.39.

The ultimate tribute you can pay the **professional** is to call him **consummate**, from the Latin, *com* , "with," and *summa*, "highest," making people carrying that adjective into "the highest altogether," for their **professions** of loyalty and commitment to a higher calling.

About those '69 Redstockings. After its first successful season, the owner, one Harry Wright, ever the **consummate professional**, moved the team, lock, stock, and barrel, to Boston. "Baseball is a business now...." he noted.

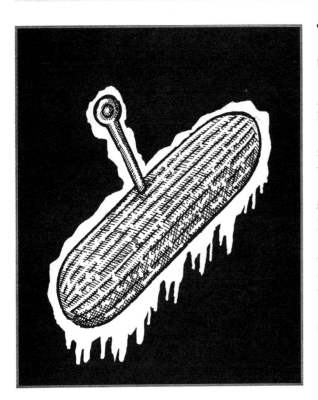

These are the **salad days** for young professional athletes, not only in the **lettuce** (c.1903) and **cabbage** (c.1903) they receive, but in the greenness of their inexperience.

Shakespeare's Cleopatra said it best, describing her admiration for Antony as, "My **salad days** when I was green in judgment, cold in blood."

All this can only leave them **in a pickle** (18thC.), "a parlous situation, predicament, or dilemma," "in a very sorry plight," "in hot water," or "on the hot seat."

The **pickle** they're **in** comes in several different varieties: **pretty**, **sad**, **fine**, or **sweet**, all from the Dutch in *de pekel zitten* "sitting in pickle juice," a brinish, vinegary liquid.

What they need to do is stay **as cool as a cucumber** (c.1732), enjoy its refreshing and cooling quality — the interior of a cucumber on a hot day being as much as twenty degrees colder than the outdoor temperature.

Rather than throwing people through windows, assaulting coaches, or kicking photographers, they might choose to emulate this rather non-spectacular vegetable and simply cool it.

The year was 217 AD. It was a warm fall day when the entire populace of an obscure English village turned out to watch hundreds of young men from two rival camps kick, push, and shove about an air-filled cow-bladder.

The mayhem which ensued proved so entertaining that the free-for all became a game held annually on special occasions such as Shrove Tuesday. When the local shoemaker fashioned a leather ball for the contest, it **kicked off** a whole new chapter in Western civilization.

During the 12th century the game was played on a large field with fifty men on a side. It was called **fut balle**, and resulted in such havoc and so many injuries that a succession of British monarchs banned the activity

The game used to be played primarily **for kicks**, a touchdown originally being the lowest score and counting for only two points. Management today **gets its kicks** from the enormous revenue it receives — as jazz musicians of the 20s got theirs from drugs. When anything threatens its source, you'll find them **kicking** loudly and publicly about it.

Legend attributes its beginnings to Abner Doubleday. It was, however, no single man's invention, evolving from games played on village greens during colonial times and went by many names — finally hitting on **baseball** in 1744.

We can credit the New York Knickerbockers for making **baseball** what it is today. Playing at Elysian Fields in 1842, "for health and recreation merely."

They brought the first real organization to the game, substituting a diamond shape for the square arrangement, pacing off the distance between bases, introducing the concept of foul territory and setting down the rules which are still with us today.

In its first years, people knew it as **the Massachusetts game** or whatever locale claimed it as its own. When **the New York rules** became the standard for the country in 1856, it became **the National game**. In the 20s and 30s, the magic bat of Babe Ruth transformed it into **the national pastime**. Walt Whitman reminded us, "It belongs as much to our institutions, fits into them as significantly as our Constitution's laws." Many have laid claim to it. One thing it's never been is "the owners game."

*O*ne of the more significant changes introduced by the New York Knickerbockers in 1845 was a rule requiring that the player be tagged with the ball or thrown out, rather than being thrown at.

This made possible the use of a harder and firmer ball, as well as ensuring greater accuracy in other phases of the game.

Organized baseball has been **playing hardball** ever since, on and off the field, making possible a tough, aggressive, no-holds-barred, no-nonsense, pull-out-all-the stops approach.

Baseball owners **play hardball** with the players, the fans, and in most recent years, with the cities whose guests they are — demanding new stadiums, under threat of departure.

If **hardball** is the body of the game, the **bunt** is its soul. The concept of giving oneself up for the good of the whole is truer to the original spirit of the game than any other strategy. It first occurred in 1872 when the Brooklyn Atlantics *butted* at the ball.

Between the instant millionaires on the field and new stadiums, built for corporate fat cats at taxpayers expense, one wonders where is the element of **sacrifice** in the game today?

When we talk baseball, we're not just playing around. We're talking serious business.

Consider the **squeeze play** (1905). As the pitch is thrown, the batter is called on to lay down a bunt as the runner on third breaks for the plate. If the batter should be unable to bunt successfully, the runner will in all probability be thrown out.

When a manager calls the **squeeze play**, he severely limits the batter's choices putting inordinate, almost unfair pressure on him to perform—a perfect model for the business world.

But you ain't seen nothin' yet. In April 1867, Candy Cummings of the Brooklyn Excelsiors unveiled a new pitch, unknown to players and fans. It caused such an uproar, it was first declared "unfair."

Harvard won the baseball championship that year led by a pitcher employing that same approach. President Charles W. Eliot of Harvard was not impressed — noting, "I am further instructed that the purpose of **the curve ball** is to deliberately deceive the batter. Harvard is not in the business of teaching deception."

But there was no holding back progress, and **throwing curveballs** and **applying squeeze plays** are now integral parts of the curricula of business and law schools everywhere, including Harvard.

Centuries ago, early hunters plucked a **feather** from the first kill of the season and proudly displayed it **in their cap**.

During Medieval times, the knights of the garter adorned their helmets with either the slender, smooth, glossy black plume of the heron's crest or an ostrich-white plume.

Worn with style and verve, the feather conveyed the **panache** for which the wearer was noted. It's that same **panache** which provides our modern day warriors, our ball players, with the style and swagger with which they play the game.

At the root of their **panache** is the Latin *penna,* "wing" or "feather," which also gave us the **pennon**, a narrow triangular cloth which flowed like a long waving plume on the lance of the medieval knight.

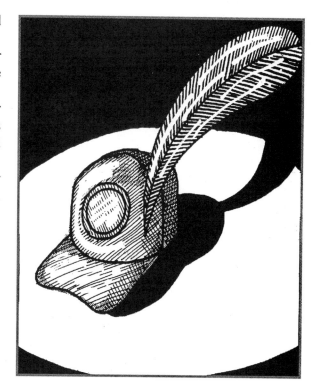

It also made for the **pinnacle**, Latin for "little wing." The word later named "a small wing-like projection above the tower of a building," hence "the top or peak of anything," before it went on to become our "highest achievement."

The highest achievement for a professional baseball team, the **pinnacle** of its season, entails securing a facsimile of the **pennon**. It takes the form of a **pennant,** that long, narrow, triangular flag flying proudly over the stadium of the winner.

ATHLETIC SUPPORTERS...

NEVERLAST

Here's to the most devoted and loyal component of organized sports — **the fan.**

He first became a sports enthusiast around 1900, probably deriving from the Latin *fanaticus,* "an overwrought or god-intoxicated person," from *fanum,* a "temple," the site of much religious fervor.

Not everyone agrees. Some find his roots instead in **fancy**, from the verb meaning "to favor."

Those of us in the know, however, consider real **fans** anything but a passing **fancy**. It is no accident that the **fan** is generally preceded by the phrase, "long suffering."

We're talking **zealots** here, from the Jewish sect locked in a life-death struggle with the Romans at Masada. With defeat imminent, Jewish defenders drew lots, selecting ten men to kill the last of their 960 comrades. One of the ten then slew the remaining nine after which he took his own life.

Zealot — an apt descriptor of any Red Sox or Cub **fan** who annually endures the agonies of hell, from the first ball thrown on opening day to the last out of each season. "Wait 'till next year," they say.

Better they too should fall on their swords.

CHAPTER 6

Transportation

THE DRIVEN PEOPLE

On September 13, 1899, Henry R. Bliss stepped off a streetcar at Central Park West and 74th Street in New York City and into the path of an automobile driven by Arthur Smith, making him the first known automobile fatality in the United States.

"Why poor Henry? "you ask.. **C'est la vie. That's how the ball bounces, the mop flops and the cookie crumbles** (all from the 50s).

That's how things happened to fall from the Latin *cadere, casu,* "fall," which via the Low Latin *cadentia*, was often applied to the throw of the dice — making for the Old French *cheance*, and allowing Mr. Bliss to take his **chances**.

Over time, things of little concern which could be left to the fall of the dice became **casual**. But when someone like Henry fell on the field of battle, things got more serious, resulting in a **casualty**.

Don't read too much into this however. All the above simply constituted an **incident** which just happened (*cadere*) "to fall" (*in*) "on" a certain date.

It was, however, a **coincidence** that Henry's arrival at that spot fell (*con*) "with" that of the auto. The position or falling (*ad*) "together" of the stars made what befell our ill-fated pedestrian into what was purely and simply an **accident** — as well as act of Bliss.

Securing a **taxi** in a major metropolitan area is never easy. Once done, hang on for dear life.

Starting life as a *taximetercabriolet,* its **capricious** nature derived from the *cabriole,* a two wheeled carriage, which in turn got its name from its bouncing and leaping motion — from the Latin *caper, capr-,* "goat."

What left you emotionally and financially spent was the **taxing** nature of the trip — from the Latin *taxare,* "to charge."

For added "measure," they included the *meter.* Any wonder we reduced it to a **taxi** or a plain old **cab**?

On August 13, 1907, the first **taximeter motor cab** took to the streets of New York City. Most New York cabs were once **Checker cabs,** sporting a bright yellow exterior with a distinctive black-and-white checker pattern. Sitting high off the road, they featured incredible leg room, spacious jump seats and extra-wide doors.

Checkers stopped manufacturing in 1982, leaving only two such **taxis** in New York operating by special dispensation from the city.

An American institution, the **Checker cab**. Hail to thee!

On August 1, 1941, Parade magazine touted the arrival of 'the army's most intriguing new gadget." Its official name was a "one and a quarter ton four-by-four command reconnaissance car." We would come to know and love it as the **jeep**.

Whence came the "**jeep?**" Some say it's merely the "G.P." for "general purpose vehicle," though it was never referred to as such. Others point to the Popeye cartoon strip by E.C. Segar and a weird little animal of that name possessed of supernatural powers who ran around squealing "**jeep!...jeep!...jeep!**"

In truth the **jeep** wasn't much of a vehicle. Awkward to maneuver, constantly leaking oil, it only rarely was able to run continuously for more than four hours.

Nonetheless, it captured the imagination and the affection of both the military and the public at large. General Eisenhower said we couldn't have won World War II without it.

Never again would we would think of cars the same way. The **jeep** begot an entire line of SUVS, UTES, Wranglers, Explorers, Broncos, and Hummers. Nothing any longer stands in our way. Across the mountains. The far side of the mall. Through the snow drifts. To Little League practice. Waiting the next adventure. The next challenge. **Jeep!... jeep!... jeep!**

Get a Horse

Into the stretch, coming round the bend they're neck and neck. Wait! Out of nowhere "It's a fiery horse with the speed of light, a cloud of dust and a Hearty Hi-Yo Silver . . ."

It's a **Garrison finish,** a spectacular come-from-behind victory at the last possible moment, against all odds! Shades of old Snapper Garrison, a 19th century American jockey, known for winning in this manner.

A real show of **horsepower.** That's what it is! Thanks to one **James Watt,** whose name adorns our monthly electric bills as **watts, kilowatts,** and **wattage** for which we pay handsome premiums.

It's he who also provided the standard for our cars, coining the term **horsepower** to indicate the output of his new steam engine — a unit of rate of work equal to the raising of 3,300 pounds one foot high in one minute.

Watt arrived at his figure by calculating that a strong dray horse averaged 2,200 foot-pounds per minute working at a gin. He then increased it by 50%, arriving at 3,300 foot-pounds which ever since has equaled one **horsepower** or 745.7 **watts.**

"Who was that Horse? Who was that masked man?" "Why don't you know? That man was . . ."

Life sure has a way of **putting you through your paces** — calling on you to display the full range of your abilities and putting you to the test.

The original **paces** were the training steps, or gaits — trot, canter, and gallop — which a horse went through, beginning in the late 18th century. Around 1871, we applied it figuratively as well as picking up the pace. That's when **speed** took on its current meaning.

Speed originally meant "success" and "good fortune," explaining all those people wishing each other "**Godspeed**." But because the race goes to the swiftest, success over time became a matter of **pace**, and the meaning of **speed** shifted to denote the pace in general and later, "rapidity."

This perhaps helps explain why you'll find so many young professionals in the **fast lane** (c.1976). Originally it was a **fast track** — an open railway route for express trains carrying perishable items and a hard and dry (hence fast) horseracing track.

Synonymous with a contemporary life style, we have high speed lanes requiring special daring and skill to negotiate. It's not without risk however. In 1955, James Dean, the promising young film star, died when his Porsche Spider went off the road, while traveling in the **fast lane.**

CHAPTER 7

Relationships

TWO TO TANGLE

I nvolved romantically? Wondering what **love's** really all about? Well...

Love's related to the Old English *leof*, "dear" or "splendid," the source of both our **leaves** and our **beliefs**.

It's not a "**love** 'em and leave 'em" phenomenon, however. This **leave** refers not to "departure" but to "permission" as in " by your leave" and "absent without leave." **Love** is a proposition by invitation only, consent first having to be granted by both parties. No one said it would be easy. As with our **beliefs**, that permission is definitely an act of faith.

The more cynical see it as part of a larger game. You know, just playing around a bit. Tennis anyone? Unfortunately, this makes **love** into nothing at all, as in the score 15-**love**.

Could **love** have originated in France with *l'oeuf,* "the egg," from its shape and being used the same way we use goose-eggs, to signify scorelessness, then corrupted later by English speaking players into **love**? It's an intriguing notion, but one on which someone laid an egg, since the French traditionally favor *zero*. Of one thing we can be sure, that when it comes to romance, few know the score. Whatever it is, it isn't **love**.

Falling Over Backwards

Would you just look at the two of them! Tripped up by their emotions, they've **head over heels in love**.

They're so confused, they've even got it backwards, **head over heels** being the way they normally are. Properly positioned, they'd be **"heels over head"** — literally doing somersaults of joy, as they did back in the 18th century.

What's so joyful about falling anyway? It generally denotes lack of control, a quick descent, disappointment, and failure — hardly the stuff of celebration.

We slip and "fall" on the ice. Our business "falls off." We even "fall from grace" — a common occurrence of the "fallen woman," though a search fails to reveal a male counterpart or his fate. The "fall guy" being but an all-purpose scapegoat.

Perhaps it's time that those romantically inclined consider the desirability of having both feet on the ground. Psychologist, Eric Fromm, suggested that it would be far better to speak of "standing firmly in love."

That's all well and good, if some solid ground can be found on which to base a relationship. Most people, however, couldn't care less, preferring the slippery slope and the prone position. Luckily their fall is generally cushioned by a tumble in the hay.

Looking for **romance**? Welcome to Rome. Where else? It's there we first heard talk of *romanice*, "in the **romantic** tongue," the street Latin spoken during the beginnings of the city — talk that would become both the syntax of **romance** languages and the stuff of future **romances**.

In Medieval times, people told lengthy verse-tales in it— stories of **derring-do** ("daring to do") centering on a knight and his lady, recounting chivalric deeds, fantastic adventures, and the agonies and ecstasies of idealized love. Thenceforth all these elements would be associated with **romance**.

Reports to the contrary, **romance** is alive and well. Only the names have been changed to protect the innocent. There's even talk of **true romance**, lending it even further cachet.

Romance, by definition, being a fictitious account, **true romance** now heads the list of prominent 20th century **oxymorons** — from the Latin *oxus,* "sharp," and *moros,* "foolish" — i.e. pointedly foolish rhetorical constructions, besting such classics as "safe sex," "deafening silence," "jumbo shrimp," and "military intelligence."

This leaves things **romantic**, once widely understood, now totally incomprehensible.

That Old Black Magic

Sound the alarms! Batten down the hatches! **Sirens** over the starboard bow! A bevy of bewitching Greek creatures, part woman, part bird, luring sailors to their death on the rocks.

The tunes they're singing are positively **enchanting,** from the Latin *incantare*, from *in*, "over," and *cantare*, "to sing;" or "chant" — as they try to "lure them over" to their side.

Initially, entailing sinister doings, it helped make an **enchantress** into a practitioner of the black arts.

Over the years, however, her evil powers waned. By the 14th century, **enchanting** someone meant simply "winning them over." This left today's **enchantress** bereft of evil. She's still bewitching and fascinating but only in a sophisticatedly benign fashion.

Think of her as **charming,** from the French *charme,* from the Latin *carmen*, a "song," or "magical incantation." A **charming** woman in 14th-century England, was considered a witch and was probably headed for trial by fire or water.

By Shakespeare's time, however, she too had lost her evil connotation. Today, we're **charmed** to simply be in her presence. **Prince Charming** is another story altogether.

Years ago you'd find him slithering about clandestinely as a **parlor snake** (c.1915) or a **lounge lizard** (c.1912).

Now he's out in the open, his status elevated to a **philanderer** (17thC.), originally a female lover of men, later a lover, and finally a "male flirt." Others know him as **libertine**, from the Roman deity *Liber*, a god of fertility whose annual celebration featured a giant wooden phallus being carted about the countryside, followed by drunken revelers who later crowned it with a wreath. There's even been talk of him as a **rake** (16thC). "You'd have to rake hell to find another like him."

An integral part of the Western literary tradition, he identifies with the greatest, including **Lothario, Casanova,** and **Don Juan.** This isn't your average **Romeo** we're talking about.

Some think him **macho,** from the Spanish *machismo* "exaggerated masculine pride," and a real cool **dude** (mid 20thC.), entering the language in 1883 as a term of ridicule for a "dandy "or a swell" — from the German *dudenkopf,* a "drowsy head." A condition that often left him **dawdling** about the bars.

Zsa Zsa Gabor wasn't impressed, noting that "**macho** does not prove mucho."

Many a man has been rendered speechless by a **glamorous** woman. Unbeknown to him, however, what he thinks is a social problem is instead a **grammatical** one.

We're not just just taking sexy syntax either. **Glamour** speaks to the mystery and power of words, and how since ancient times, those in possession of verbal skills have limited their access, creating an almost supernatural aura about them.

When scholars made Latin the language of the cultured few, the bulk of the populace accredited occult and devilish powers to those fluent in the language and its **grammar**.

Through usage, the "r" in **grammar** changed to an "l." A few other modifications and voila! A new word, **glamour,** but one which retained the magical sense of its predecessor. Accordingly, the first meaning of the new word was a "spell," or a "charm."

Grammar has long since lost its charm for students, though it continues to magically evoke sleep in them.

Grown men meanwhile labor to complete a sentence while under the spell of the **glamorous** woman.

If we all had only listened to our seventh grade English teacher.

There sure are lots of **attractive** people out there. If we can believe all the "**Attractive** DWF, HWP, seeks M..." personals.

Defying truth in advertising, the word has in it both elements of **traction** — "the act of drawing or pulling" and **tract**, "a "declaration" or "appeal." Both derive from the Latin *attrahere,* "to draw towards," providing the **attraction** which for many has proven fatal.

That one over there! Stunning!...just **gorgeous**! She looks good enough to devour. And why not? She could derive from the Late Latin *gorga*, "throat," causing us to **gorge** ourselves, **gurgle**, and **regurgitate**. There's also the Old French *gorgias*, "a neckpiece" — yet another fancy item.

While you're at it, check out that **handsome** guy! **Handsome** is one of the few words we have to describe a romantic man. A real hands-on characterization, **handsome** originally meant "dextrous," "manually apt," "honest," "and "straightforward." "**Handsome is as handsome does**," we used to say.

Only recently have some of the **attractive** people rediscovered that the real basis of any **attraction** is what people do, not how they look. The majority continue to rely on the luck of the draw.

Splitting Hairs

Hair pinned atop the head once spoke to a certain dignity and reserve. **Letting it down** showed you relaxed and uninhibited.It could also lead to a **bad hair day** (1991) on which the sorry state of your hair accurately reflected your miserable state of mind.

For that king-size hangover we suggest a little **of the hair of the dog**, "whatever made you drunk or sick the previous night." This from the Ancient folk treatment for a dog-bite, placing a burnt hair of the dog that bit you directly on the wound. It's a variation of the basic homeopathic principle, *similia similibus, curantur,* "likes are cured by likes."

Hair has long had magical powers attributed to it. In many cultures, it's also considered highly erotic. Hence the big cover-up there.

During the 19th century we spoke of men **feeling hairy**, "having a must" — running around looking for **a bit of hair**. All they wanted was to **get a haircut** to relieve the urgency. A crewcut? A little off behind the ears?

The Puritans introduced the modern short haircut to the world as well as their suffocating sexual strictures. Given the results, maybe it's worth the risk and **let it all hang out**.

Defining the word **sex** represents one of the more formidable tasks of our time. Let's try.

Sex comes from the Latin *secare*, "to cut or divide" — our first use of the word designating the two major categories of humanity we have come to know and love as male and female.

According to Greek mythology, we began life as a perfect four-armed and-legged he/she unit. Unfortunately we were so taken with ourselves that we offended the mighty Zeus who proceeded to sever us into two separate entities.

We later used the word not only to divide the **sexes**, but to describe the primary qualities of being male or female. This unfortunately led to the male being referred to as "the better" and the "sterner" **sex**; the female as "the fairer," "the gentler," "the softer," and "the devout" **sex**. Women were also called "the second **sex**," further underscoring the division.

To address the problem, we began using **sex** to help forge a new togetherness, a way of finally getting our act together.

Today, **having sex** (20th C.) literally speaks to that unifying process.

Indeed!

In an era of sexual enlightenment, many believe there's little room for the **prude**.

Her **proud** lineage, however, calls for closer examination. An offspring of the Latin *prodesse,* "to be useful or advantageous," she moved into Old French as *prod,* "good," "gallant," or "brave," evolving over time into *le prud'homme,* the "honest and upright man" and *la prudefemme,* the "strong and modest woman."

The language, however, couldn't tolerate a *prud* woman, and her modesty and strength soon gave way to excessive propriety and priggishness.

Ostensibly genderless, the **prude** today is seen primarily as a woman — victim of the same sexism in language that transformed the good **housewife** into a **hussy**.

Must a woman be a **prude** in order to maintain her **pride?** She can take comfort and strength from the word's original meaning as well as being **prudent**.

Being **prudent,** however, has nothing to do with being a **prude**. She became **prudent** by shortening the present participle *providens,* "foreseeing" into *prudens,* "wise," or "discreet" — something of which both men and women may feel **proud**.

The Viagra craze demonstrates the lengths to which some men will go to spice up their life.

Guys everywhere are turning to their their pharmacist to add that something special to their otherwise non-descript existence. Consider it a bit of **relish,** from the Old French *relais,* "remainder" — the aftertaste that turns an ordinary meal into a delicacy.

Nothing new here. What men have traditionally **relished** is being **the mustard**, "the genuine article or the main attraction," (19th C.), while traditionally linking the ability to **cut the mustard** to their sexual prowess.

Over time, they extended its meaning to "meeting or exceeding performance requirements," whatever the challenge — adding the refrain "If you can't **cut the mustard**, you can at least lick the jar."

Mustard is a fine flavor enhancer. Like all such spices, it's best to **cut it** first, adding it to the food in very small amounts.

But how much talent does it really take to **cut the mustard**? Could they instead be just trying to **pass muster**, like a soldier during inspection? Either way, guys, you're not up for inspection, and mustard is merely the finishing touch, not the main meal, no matter how you **cut it**.

Words fail when it comes to describing unmarried people living together.

In the 19th century, they did it **without benefit of clergy,** which originally described denial of the last rites to one who had committed suicide. Why not? You might as well have been dead, living in sin as you were.

By the roaring twenties, things loosened up somewhat. Traveling salesmen and truckers began **shacking up** with local girls to meet their needs away from home, as did soldiers during W.W.II — until **shacking up** became synonymous with out and out promiscuity.

It's now relatively easy to earn the Good Housekeeping Seal of Approval. Just **enter into a primary relationship** with a **significant other**(1980s). For one so **significant**, however, the **other** remains nondescript. Politics, in the form of the U.S. Census Bureau, made for the strangest bedfellow of all.

After years of struggling with "partner" and "roommate," it finally came up with the **POSSLQ,** a "person of the opposite sex sharing living quarters". They, however, overlooked the **PSSSLQ.** Either way, have you hugged your **PO(S)SSLQ** today?

What's cool today? Getting your **thrills** by piercing body parts — everything from earlobes to navels and labiae and all stops betwixt and between — from the Middle English *thrillen*, " to perforate with a pointed instrument."

It's perfectly natural that you and your partner get off on this romantically. When **thrilled** to the core, you are "pierced" by a sudden, intense emotion, resulting in pleasure and delight. Ouch!

Cheap **thrills?** Nothing links two people more closely together than getting their nose rings entangled. On a simpler level, a **nostril** was originally a *nosthirl*, literally, "a hole drilled in the nose."

Make sure you top it all off with a few **tattoos,** from Polynesia or perhaps Tahiti or Samoa.

Don't confuse your personal **tattoo**, however, with the military **tattoo,** a signal calling soldiers to their quarters at night. This came from the Dutch *taptoe* — from *tap*, the "faucet of a cask, "and *toe*, "shut." This **tattoo** referred to a police visit to taverns in the evening for the purpose of shutting off the **taps** of the casks (c.1780).

Cold beer **on tap?** With thoughts of that and the sound of **taps** echoing in the background, we beat a hasty retreat.

Making a Clean Breast

We've been **bosom friends** since the end of the 16th century, but it took W.W.II to make us **bosom buddies** — from **buddy's** common use as a synonym for a "pal" in the armed services.

Every guy needs a **buddy,** a mid 19th century variation of *butty companion* — from the *booty fellow*, an associate with whom you shared your plunder.

The **bosom's** the perfect place to carry your friendships, because of its proximity to the heart and its innocuous nature. In the middle of the 19th century, breasts fell out of favor and "nice" people stopped referring to them. When invited out for turkey dinner, and you wanted some white meat, you always asked for the turkey **bosom**, never the breast.

Over time, the breast came to be perceived as increasingly impolite to the point of being considered savage, and the **bosom**, as refined and gentle.

Though **bosoms** had a brief wild fling as *bazooms* (mid 20th C.), they ultimately reverted to their conservative character and traditional spelling.

At a time when acceptable words are hard to come by, the **bosom's** there for you. Here's to the **bosom** and all its friends.

FRIENDS BREAKING BREAD...

Would you believe this guy? For years we've been keeping **company** — literally breaking bread together from the Latin *com*, "with," and *panis*, "bread." And the best he can say is "we're good **friends**!"

Not to fret. A **friend** is about as good as it gets. He originated in early Anglo-Saxon times when households were divided into your loved ones, those related by blood or marriage, and the slaves for whom you couldn't care less.

A favorite word of the time was *freon*, "to love." But because you couldn't possibly love someone you held in bondage, **free**, meaning "beloved" also came to mean "not slave" — **free** in the modern sense of the word. It thus insured that all future **friendships** would be based on both "**freedom**" and "love."

Free and love are two of the most beautiful words in the English language. How appropriate that when all else fails, it comes down to them, and that they both come down to being a good **friend**.

CHAPTER 8

Marriage

HOMEWORK

He was your happy-go-lucky bachelor, often listed in Medieval Registers as Latin *solutus*, "loose or unchained." This made him **footloose**, "unfettered," **and fancy free**, "with nary a romantic commitment" (early 20thC.).

He came upon this ravishing woman in a bar. She absolutely **enthralled** him. *Thrall* is Anglo Saxon for "slave." When you *enthrall* another, you "reduce him to the condition of a *thrall*" — in short, you enslave him. Soon he was a "prisoner of love."

He agreed to **tie the knot** (11th C.), further underscoring the entanglement. But what's a rope when you have **wedlock**?

To Lord Byron "A **wedlock** and a padlock mean the same thing." Not really. The Old English *weddian* was a "pledge," and that **lock** was really a *lac* or "gift," our first **wedlock** being the present given at the time the pledge of marriage was made, helping seal the engagement.

Now things appear **deadlocked** (1778), "at a complete standstill," a term that preceded the "springless lock that opens with a key."

Though outstanding issues may eventually be resolved, there are no guarantees of closure. According to your local bookie, a **lock** (1940s) is a "sure thing", an "absolute certainty." Marriage, a **lock**? Forget it!

*A*fter the divorce, and all the spoils have been divvied up, comes the realization that marriage is truly a contractual relationship.

In Ancient Greece, businessmen traditionally consummated the signing of a contract by pouring wine on the altar of the gods. The word for this was *spendo*, " to pour out a libation," which because of its association with business, came to mean "to make an agreement."

In Latin, it begot *spondere*, *spons-*, "to speak or pledge," helping a couple **espouse** their love for one another. This led to his becoming a *sponsus*, "one who promised something" — making him a "betrothed man," and her a *sponsa*, a "betrothed woman."

Because of the promises made, both later appeared in English as one another's **spouse**. A source of joy initially, these same promises left them **despondent** afterwards when they moved *de*, "away from" them.

A word from our **sponsor**: Long before it meant "to pledge," to wed also meant "to gamble" All bets were off, however, when someone later *weddian* another, "for fairer, for fouler." Today, the **wedding** is still a gamble, but it's no longer explicit — the risk lurking surreptitiously behind the promises.

*G*etting down to basics, today we're talking **bread and butter** issues.

Bread and butter has been our "livelihood" since the early 18th century. In fact, from the mid 18th to the early 19th century, being **out of bread** made us "out of work." **Bread's** also been "money," since about 1935, having been properly preceded by **dough** as early as 1851.

Bread also defined our roles as men and women. *Hlaf* was Old English for a "loaf of bread." In perhaps the meanest cut of all, it created the *hlaefdig,* "the loaf-kneader" — from *dey,* a "worker" or "server," helping make a **Lady** of her. The *hlaefwerad,* the "keeper or guardian of the loaf," made him her **Lord**.

This was in keeping with the long standing notion of man as the **breadwinner**, from the Anglo Saxon *winnan,* to "toil." Because hard work usually pays off, **winning** eventually came to mean "striving with positive results."

It usually takes some **dough** to get the **breadwinner** off his **duff** (mid 20th C.) — the *gh* in **dough** once having been pronounced like an "f," the word itself meaning the "soft or spongy part of anything."

Making it time perhaps for milady to kick some buns.

Family argument about to turn violent? Before you lift a hand to strike, why don't you first try and **strike a balance**.

Imagine a set of scales, allowing you the opportunity to achieve a position between the two extremes — providing a balanced perspective by simply lending equal weight to each side.

Doing so might enable you to **strike a bargain**. Ancient Greeks and Romans customarily sealed a business contract by **striking** or killing an animal and offering it up to the deities.

What are you willing to sacrifice to keep the peace? It could be nothing more than saying the right word. Doing so could **strike the right chord**, from the French *accorder* which derives from *corda*, "a harp-string."

When you strike a string of a musical instrument that is finely tuned, it will make any string tuned to the same pitch vibrate sympathetically. It should enable you to not only strike the right note but also hit **a sympathetic chord** — allowing you and your partner to once again make beautiful music together.

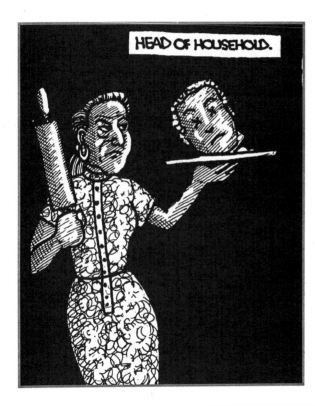

HEAD OF HOUSEHOLD.

Hello there. This is your captain speaking. Your **father.** The head of the household. The first and last word on every subject. **Father knows best**.

This was further underscored in 1949 when the show of the same name made its NBC radio debut with Robert Young in the title role.

Every **father** has his roots in the Latin *pater, patr-*. making him also into a *patronus*, a "support," "guardian," "protector," and "model."

Our Father which art in heaven created man in his own image. So our earthly **father**, in the execution of his duties, provides the **pattern** or "model" for his family. This includes his role as **patron** at shopping centers through the proxy of his wife and children. Though such **patronage** makes him quite lovable, his **patronizing** nature also puts many off.

The extension of **fatherhood** made for *patria*, the "fatherland" which helped make us **patriotic**. It also created the popular but ill-fitting **paternity suit**, showing that fatherhood can also be the last refuge of a scoundrel.

In the family, like any organization, it's the person at the top who really counts. What's that you want? ... I'm sorry. I leave those decisions to my wife... Mother!!!!

Though ours is the era of the strong-willed woman, there's little talk of the **henpecked** man.

Centuries ago, however, writers were obsessed with him. Butler noted how "The **henpeck** man rides behind his wife and lets her wear the spurs and govern the reins." Poor Dryden bemoaned his own fate, "Was ever poor deity so **hen-pecked** as I am!" And Steele proclaimed Socrates "the head of the Sect of the **Hen-Pecked**."

Henpeckery was first validated in a famous study done by W.C.Allen in the 1920s showing how stronger birds asserted their authority over the weaker ones. Once a chicken established its position in the **pecking order**, it had to submit to those above, but could peck freely at the others below.

Hens rarely peck at the rooster. He is, after all, the **cock of the walk.** His fighting instinct has been honed to perfection, and he knows it. Many men model themselves after him, hoping to emulate his **cocksure attitude**. Most end up just out-and-out **cocky.**

If you're looking for a marriage that's **impeccable**, " free from faults" — from the Latin *im*, "not "and *peccare*, "to sin," you have only to stay away from affairs and those tasty **peccadilloes**.

Many know a **woman** only as a wife and mother and in relation to her household duties.

A certain Samuel Purchase surmised back in 1619 that she is "a house builded for generation and gestation, whence our language calls her **woman**, "womb-man." But if a **woman** is a womb, what does it make a man?

Other male linguists were even nastier, arguing that she was "a woe to man." More likely she was a **wifman**(c.766), a compound of *wif* + *man*, "human being," the *wif* deriving from the Anglo Saxon *wifan*, "to weave," her work in the household primarily defining her as a person.

A single woman helped change that. Mary Hays McCauley was a water carrier at the battle of Monmouth in 1778. Beloved and respected by the soldiers in the field, Molly Pitcher, as she came to be known, was not only a wife, mother, baker, and weaver, but also a heroine who so distinguished herself during the course of battle that General Washington made her a non-commissioned officer, the first woman to receive such an honor.

We didn't hear of a **woman's rights** until 1840, and **women's rights** until 1850. **Women's Liberation** was delayed until 1966. It's surely time we heard more of "Sergeant Molly."

Atribute to a **virtual** unknown — Annie Peck, for attaining great heights. In 1895, she scaled the Matterhorn; later, Mt. Huascaren — the highest peak in the Western hemisphere, ever climbed by anyone. At age 61, she scaled Mt. Coropuna in Peru (21,250 feet), planting a "Votes for Women" banner at the summit.

These courageous feats of strength unfortunately can only be measured against those of a man. In Latin he was *vir*, "a male adult." His "masculine strength," came from the Latin *virilis,* "manly," helping him to not only establish his **virility**, but to define his *virtus* — his "worth," or "excellence."

Moral excellence later made him **virtuous**. When applied to a woman, it simply left her "chaste."

The **virile** man may be full of **vim**, from the Latin for "force." Misuse of that force, however, also created much of the **violence** in the world, from *violentus*, "impetuous" or "boisterous" — leading to his **violation** of both laws and women, from *violare, violatus*, "to maltreat or dishonor." As to the **virtuous** female, all we have left today is the **virago**, a "noisy, domineering woman." Better we return to Ancient Rome where she was "a heroic woman or "a female warrior." A perfect description of an Annie Peck.

Alas, the Roman had to add, "strong and brave as a man."

Mother's day is the day for all mothers. It's also **the mother of all days** — thanks to Saddam Hussein who used the phrase, *ummm al-ma' arik,* "the mother of all battles," during the Gulf war, "mother" being an Arabic figure of speech for "major," or the "greatest."

Copy writers here pounced on the phrase. Sooner than you could say "pepperoni," we were ordering **the mother of all pizzas**.

We celebrated our first **mother's day** on May 10, 1910 in Philadelphia Pennsylvania, thanks to one Anna Jarvis who proposed the name as well as a ritual which entailed the wearing of a carnation in honor of ones mother — red if she were alive, white, if she had passed away. The custom went on to become an integral part of the day for the next forty years, making one wonder how FTD ever missed out on this one.

We celebrate many things that day — not only individual mothers, but also the generative principle, love, and nurturing. A popular song in 1900 was "Daddy, You've Been a Mother to me." Mothers and mothering come in many forms. So to all you mas, moms, MAmas, MaMAs,and mommies everywhere — regardless of your sex — a happy **mother's day**, not just on that day, but on every day of the year

We've been **saving our bacon** since the 16th century by "escaping injury" or "avoiding a loss." Given how bacon was such a precious commodity, elaborate precautions were always taken in storing it for the winter — especially keeping it out of the reach of house dogs.

Meanwhile we continued to **bring home the bacon** — simply earning a living and providing our family with the necessities of life. It also helped us to "succeed in a given enterprise" or "win the prize" (1925). This from county fairs and their greased pig contests, where whoever caught the pig, got to keep it—literally **bringing home the bacon**.

Another story, however, gets the prize. In the first years of the 12th century, a unique custom began in Dunmow, a village in Essex, England, called "the awarding of the flitch." A flitch, or side of bacon, was offered annually to any person who would kneel at the church door and swear that he and his wife had not quarreled at any time during the preceding year nor had they during that time ever wished themselves unmarried.

Records show that from 1244 until 1722 when the contest ceased — a period of almost 300 years — couples had **brought home the bacon** a grand total of five times.

When we were boys the world was good
But that is long ago:
Now all the wisest folks are lewd,
for **adultery's** the go
The go, the go
Adultery's the go.
—— Victorian Ditty

When the Air Force and the Army took a hard line on **adultery**, they equated defense of our country with defense of conventional morality.

How defensible is their meddling in actions involving freely consenting **adults**? Supporters note how **adultery's** not only not **adult** behavior; it's not even **adolescent**. **Adult** and **adolescent** both derive from the Latin *ad* and *alere*, "to nourish or raise towards maturity." Moralists argue as to how **adultery** comes from *ad* and *alterare*, "to change into something else," as "to corrupt another." Be that as it may, nothing's been more corrupted than the word **adult** which now connotes a wide range of behavior that is puerile.

The war on **adultery**? It's so childish as to drive one to an **adult-entertainment zone** for some **adult** reading matter.

CHAPTER 9

We and They

THE OTHER HALF

Two, four, six, eight, whom do we appreciate? People who are our **kind** of people, that's who.

It's all pretty obvious. The Gothic *kuni* made for our **kin,** while also making us **kind** (pronounced initially with a short "i"), an attitude we generally reserved for our **kinfolk**.

Similarly, the Latin *genus, gener,* "breed" or "kin," left us **generous**, "full of the spirit of our group," and *gignere, gent-,* besides helping us **beget**, spawned the **genius** in us, "the guardian spirit of the group." It also left us **gentle**, "of that group," **congenial**, "with the group," warning us of the **degeneracy** that comes of falling "from the group."

Those whom we truly appreciate are those who are our **spittin' image** (also **spit in image**, **spitting image**, and **spitten image**) — so much like us, we could conceivably have been spit from their mouth. Though it's unlikely anyone had any knowledge of DNA back in the 15th century when the phrase was first uttered. More likely, it's a corruption of "spirit and image," comparing one's energy and looks with another.

In keeping with the spirit of things, the **kind** thing to do is to now show some of that same **generosity** and **congeniality** to others as well as to our own **kind**.

What makes for all the **bigotry** in the world? It's a pretty hairy topic. Our first **bigots** were themselves victims of **bigotry** based on their physical appearance.

The Spanish *hombre de bigote* was literally, a "bearded man." Though his countrymen saw him as a fiery and spirited fellow, others experienced him as a zealot.

No isolated incident, early in their history, the clean shaven French applied the word *bigoz* to their enemies whose hairy faces they disliked.

Over time, the **bigot** switched roles from the object of prejudice to its active subject. No wonder that the word was long synonymous with a "hypocrite," there being a thin line between being a **bigot** and calling someone else one.

If you think that's **bizarre**, you're correct. To the Basques, *bizarra* was the beard worn by their warriors whose dashing and debonair character made them *bizarro* — "handsome and brave." When others saw these hirsute characters charging with swords drawn, they became "fearful," and "awesome," then "strange," and finally, "outlandish" and "grotesque."

Does that make escaping from a **bizarre** enemy into a close shave? Only the **bigots** know for sure.

It's the time of the Athenian city-state, and you're a stranger in a strange land.

The language of the Athenians sounds, well, Greek to you. Your speech is also undecipherable to them. Whenever you open your mouth, all they hear is "bar-bar-bar," something akin to "blah-blah-blah." This makes for *barbaros,* a "stammering" and turns you into a **barbarian.** People were distrustful and suspicious of the **barbarians.** As every good citizen of Athens knew, anyone who didn't speak Greek was capable of the most heinous and uncivilized acts.

Long after the heyday of Athenian culture, **barbarism** came to refer to the mixing of foreign words with Greek or Latin. Our new **barbarians** were uncultured persons, poor boobs who were not totally conversant with the classical languages. How **barbaric** can you get! Clearly, they were but a few steps removed from immorality and violence.

Today, anyone different is a prospective **barbarian. Savages** is what they are, from *silvaticus,* one living in *silva,* the woods. Jean Jacques Rousseau confused matters with *le noble sauvage* — leaving us wondering who are the **barbarians** currently **savaging** the environment.

*E*veryone at the party but you got the hot hors d'oeuvres. All you got were the day-old leftovers and the **cold shoulder**. Was the hostess saying something by her actions?

It's a culinary message first recorded by Sir Walter Scott, noting how a hostess would serve a hot meat to a welcome guest, offering a **cold shoulder** of mutton instead to those who were unwelcome or had overstayed their visit.

If you think you were **snubbed**, you're correct, having been "cut short," as in the original meaning of the word, like the **snub** noses turned up at you.

Those **snobs** wouldn't be so haughty if they knew their true origins, starting life as 18th century cobblers and going on to later become synonymous with the entire lower class.

Their lowly status was certified at Cambridge where commoners admitted to the University were required to put *sine nobilite,* "without nobility," next to their name — a phrase which was eventually shortened to *"s. nob."*

Quick to turn class distinctions on their head, the victims, once having achieved a higher status, began flaunting the designation, showing others the same disdain and contempt that had been visited upon them, creating the **snobs** whom we know today.

Beats Me

They started in Bohemia as the gypsies of Eastern Europe. By 1910, they were synonymous with those who didn't fit in — like the non-conforming, scandalously immoral artists of Greenwich village. Not without redeeming value, **Bohemians** were in some quarters considered **hep** (1903), "informed" or "knowledgeable."

Hep slipped into **hip** (1931), jazzmen making for **hip cats** dating cool chicks. Those "in the know" were definitely **hip**.

Hip extended itself during 1945-55 with the emergence of the **hipsters** who in turn spawned the **Beat generation** (1957). Ginsberg and Kerouac were its prime exemplars. Its foundlings were **beatniks** — one of the many **-ik** words spun off the launch of the Soviet *Sputnik* (a "traveling companion.").

Serious **beats** begot the anti-establishment brats known as **hippies** and **rebels without a cause**, from the title of Robert Lindner's book (1954) and the popular James Dean movie (1955).

Tie-dyed, adorned with love beads, sandals, and granny glasses, they founded the **Woodstock Nation** on August 15, 1969 at 7:00 A.M. on a dairy pasture in upper New York state. In '68 came the **Yippies,** the Youth International Party of Rubin and Hoffman, transmogrifying into today's **Yuppies** — truly the children our parents warned us against.

Drumming Up Support

A certain 19th century lawyer acquired a herd of cattle in payment of a debt. Not much of a rancher, he failed to carefully tend his stock —not even making the effort to brand it properly. His cattle ended up all over the place, often mingling with that of other ranchers.

Whenever the issue of ownership of a stray was in question, his men simply invoked the name of the owner. "They're **Maverick's**," they would say. By the middle of the century, Samuel **Maverick's** name was linked forever with those who stray from the herd, following the dictates of their own conscience.

Some think **mavericks** to be odd or eccentric. Henry David Thoreau reminded us however: "If one man in a marching column is out of step, it may look as if he is marching to the best of another drummer. Let him step to the music which he hears, however measured or far away."

It's not without risk however. Far away, In India, the *Pariayer* was a caste that derived its name from the Tamil *parai* — huge drums they beat on at religious festivals. When the British occupied India, they drew heavily upon this group to perform their menial work. Their name as well as their spirit was corrupted, ending up describing any despised person or outcast, resulting in our **pariahs**.

Anti-war sentiment peaked on October 10, 1967 as hundreds of **protesters** stormed the Pentagon. Their actions put Democracy sorely to the test and divided the country.

Supporters saw their **protests** primarily as a **testament** to their courage. It does, after all, take *cojones* to bear witness or **testify** on behalf of ones convictions.

Cojones is Spanish for **testicles** (c.1425) which derive from the Latin *testes*, "witness" and *testiculs*, "little witness" — it once being customary for men to pledge faith or swear **testimony** by holding or touching one another's genitals.

You'll find reference to it in the Old Testament in I Chronicles 29:24 where the Captains of Israel take hold of Solomon's as a gesture of loyalty as well as in Genesis 24:9 where the servant — out of deference to the verbally fearful — "placed his hands on Abraham's thighs."

Student **protests** were a positive **testimony**, *pro*, "for" the beliefs they held, their actions **attesting** or serving as personal **testimony** *ad*, "towards" them.

To this day, however, there are those who **detest** the **protesters** and who would bear witness against them, **testifying** so — *de* "from" the very bottom of their you-know-whats.

*O*de to the **square**. In an era marked by distrust and unpredictability, it's nice to know that a few bastions of reliability remain.

We start from **square one**, as in a board game, beginning with the Masons who used the **square's** right angle to properly set bricks. This created upright people, those "on the level" who did **things on the square,** "in a fair and even-handed manner," leaving us **square with each other**.

As the orchestra conductor's hand beats out a regular and unsyncopated four-beat rhythm, delineating a square, **squaring things** helped set things right (late 19thC.).

It also produced the **square shooter** (early 20thC.), noted for his honesty and candor, as well as making for the **square meal,** "one that is hearty and fulfilling." Any wonder we crave our **three squares** every day?

A social misfit during the 40s, the counterpart of today's nerd, the **square** and his lifestyle have often been the subject of mockery. But he's now due some respect.

We have our circle of friends, a love triangle, and occasionally a little something on the side, but what ultimately figures are people who are **square** with us.

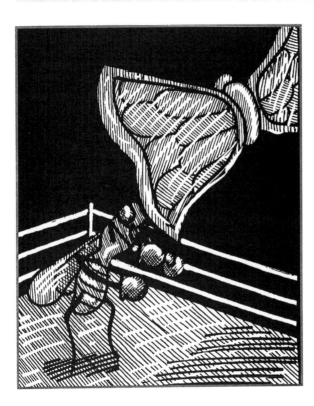

On September 4, 1960 a young boxer named Cassius Clay from Louisville, Kentucky won a gold medal at the Olympic Games in Rome.

Four years later, now known as Muhammad Ali, he became world heavyweight champion, proclaiming "I am the greatest,...the prettiest" — verbiage he later admitted to having pilfered from a popular wrestler of the time, named "Gorgeous George."

Ali's style in the ring was to "float like a butterfly, sting like a bee." Outside the ring, he floated effortlessly through interviews, stinging many a reporter in the process and earning him the title of "The mouth."

It would not be **tangential** to say this was a man who also survived many battles outside the ring with grace and bravado. He did so with principles **intact** — from the Latin *in*, "not" and *tactus*, "touched", the past participle of *tangere*, "to touch." This made Ali an **integral** part of the sixties, a figure without whom that period would not be complete — a man of **integrity**, one "sound and whole." Adding *de,* "away from" to *videre*, to see," enables us to see things **divided,** "apart from one another."

Ali will always be seen as an **individual**, "one **undivided**." Together, unique, one of a kind — he was truly "The greatest."

As I Live and Breathe

What does it take to be a creative person? What goes into the making of a **genius**?

Some think it's a matter of divine **inspiration**. The Romans believed that **inspiration** came from the gods breathing into your being, combining the Latin *in*, "into" with *spirare*, "to breathe." Thomas Edison, on the other hand, emphasized the hard work you put into it, namely the **perspiration,** a "breathing, *per,* "through" the skin."

Enthusiasm counts. It too is God blessed, from the Greek *enthousiasmos* from *en,* "in" and *thousiasmos*, "god," together creating your "god within."

In Ancient Rome every man and woman was said to receive a "tutelary god" or "attendant spirit" at birth. This spirit served as their protector throughout life, governed their fortune, shaped their character and, finally, conducted them out of this world. Women knew this spirit as their **Juno**; men referred to it as their **genius**.

Now, don't you think it's time we finally acknowledged the **genius** in each of us?

Perhaps, in keeping with the Arabic *djin/jinni* or **genie**, we might no longer keep that **genius** of ours bottled up.

Getting A Head

Phrenology was a 19th century pseudo-science linking a person's intelligence and temperament to the shape of his head.

Individuals with a high brow and high forehead were said to have a larger brain, making for the **highbrow** (1875), the intellectually and culturally superior person. In 1902, he was joined by the **lowbrow**, "an individual with no breeding and negligible mental capacity," and in the 1940s, by the **middlebrow,** "one of mediocre intelligence and bourgeois tastes" — first introduced to us in *Life* magazine.

You can instantly recognize the **highbrow** by his disdain for others, shown by his lifting of an eyebrow. *Cilium* is Latin for "eyelash;" *super,* "above." What's above the eyelash is the eyebrow. Adding the suffix *ous* made him "full of eyebrow" or **supercilious**.

Adlai Stevenson batted nary an eyelash, while bearing the label "**egghead**" during the presidential campaign of 1952. To his numerous critics he remarked, "**Eggheads** of the world, unite; you have nothing to lose but your yolks."

This can only lead to a **supercilious** comment as to how **highbrows** find their solace in bad humor, while **lowbrows** find theirs in Rogaine.

Duh!

Time for a little **morology** (16th-17thC.) — some "foolish talk." It's no simple task, since people ceased being stupid and became "mentally challenged."

It hasn't always been that way. As noted by wordsmith Joseph Shipley, **moron** has the distinction of being the only word formally voted into the English language. Derived from the Greek *moros*, "stupid," it was formally adopted in 1910 by the American Association for the Study of the Feeble-Minded — also a no-no today.

If it seems **idiotic**, that's alright. The Greek *idiotes*, were just "private persons," those who did not hold public office — from *idios*, "individual." Under the Romans, they became "those unfit for political life" and eventually, "those mentally deficient."

One of the **idiosyncrasies** (*idios*, "private"+ *syn*, "together," +*crasis*, a "combination") of our culture is that only an **idiot** would run for public office. Many intelligent people avoid politics altogether.

Don't even vote? Citing a popular **idiom** — "an expression "peculiar to the language"— the sage, Homer Simpson once asked, "Are you squandering the precious gift of life sitting in front of the **idiot box**?" Now that's truly **idiotic**!

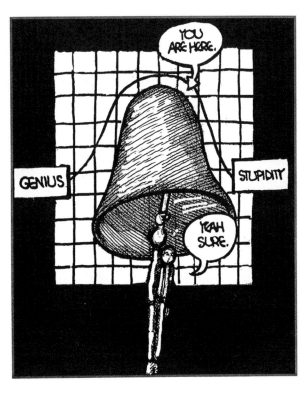

*O*ur culture lives and dies by the bell—the bell curve. Tolling success and failure for the masses, it sorts the **ding-a-lings** and **dumbbells** from the **ringers**.

Our first **dumbbells** were simply the apparatus used to ring church bells without sound, helping trainees learn to chime without going deaf in the process. They later provided exercise as dead weights at your health club. As you can see, they're not without value.

Ringers have long been identified with the real thing. Historically, they're items whose true value has been disguised, such as counterfeit coins. They were easily tested. When struck on a hard surface, authentic coins produced a vibrant sound, **ringing true**. Bogus coins produced dull, flat tones, **ringing hollow** — as do the arguments for testing and the bell curve.

Because even the slightest imperfection affects its tone, **being sound as a bell** means you are in peak condition. There's little sound about the bell curve — there being little correlation between IQ scores and creativity and having a successful life.

What does **ring true** is the specific characteristics the individual brings to the life experience, the sum total of which most fully resonate for him or her.

What Kind of Fool Am I?

Here's to the **fool.** Courtesy of the Latin *follis*, "bellows" or "windbag," he once named the French court jester, the *fol*, who carried an air filled bladder tied to the end of a stick with which he flayed members of his audience.

In the plural he was synonymous with puffed cheeks — often depicted as the wind, for the tricks it played. This was nothing, however, compared to all the **folly** he contributed.

We have mixed feelings about the **fool.** The joker is, after all, wild. We feel **foolish** after having done something stupid, but invariably find ourselves **fooling around** — experimenting and striking out in new directions.

Though we enjoy deceiving people, especially those in positions of authority, by **making fools of them**, we plead with them afterwards that we be taken seriously by saying "**no fooling.**"

After the Norman conquest of England in 1066, the victorious Normans had nothing to do but hunt and play. They were *selie*, "blessed." Gradually, the word came to mean "idle." With the growth of industrialism, it became outright **foolish**.

April Fool's Day, which dates back to Ancient Rome, celebrates that **foolishness** — a reminder that it is we the **silly** who shall inherit the earth.

September 23, 1908. The pennant is on the line as the Chicago Cubs meet the New York Giants at the Polo Grounds.

The Giants regular first baseman is laid up with an injury, forcing manager, John McGraw to play a promising nineteen year old named Fred Merkle in his place.

With two outs in the bottom of the ninth, the score tied, and the winning run on third and Merkle on first, the Giant hitter lashes a single, sending the runner on third home with the winning score. Merkle crosses the plate, but forgets to touch second, is eventually tagged out, and his run doesn't count. The game is later ruled a tie, resulting in a playoff game which the Cubs win, sending them to the world series. The press unleashes its fury. A New York sportswriter dubs the ill-fated Merkle a "**bonehead**" — making his play into **the Merkle boner** and forever memorializing him as a **dunce**.

John Duns Scotus was a brilliant 13th century philosopher, but his followers were doctrinaire hairsplitters. They became *Dunsmen,* a term originally synonymous with "over refinement" and "pedantry".

As today's **dunces**, they're real **dunderheads** — from the Dutch *donderbol*, "cannonball," in reference to their hard heads, and destined like poor Merkle, to live on in ignominy for their base deeds.

CHAPTER 10

Altruism

DOING UNTO OTHERS

A Real Croc

Mo feigning sympathy here. No way you're getting over on us by **crying crocodile tears** (15thC.).

Myth has it that the reptile sheds tears, attracting the attention and sympathy of passersby who, when they get close enough, are pounced upon and devoured, the croc's tears flowing unabatedly all the while.

The facts are that big crocodiles — the Indo-Pacific species is about 23 feet long and 2,000 pounds — don't cry. In fact, the smaller ones don't either.

What then about his little brother indigenous to China and North America? He's just a lizard. "About the size of a forearm," or *lagarto,* said the Spaniards—who, on first encountering a giant variety of the species, added *el* for emphasis, creating *el lagarto,* whom we later corrupted into an **alligator**.

Both the large and small species are endangered. So **see you later alligator** — courtesy of British rhyming slang of the 1850s that enjoyed a renaissance in the 1930s and 40s, musicians describing fellow jazzmen as **alligators**. This was later underscored by Bill Haley and the Comets' 50s hit, "**See You Later Alligator.**"

The response? "**In a while** or **on the Nile, crocodile**"

Anything but tears.

Portia faces life "…a story reflecting the courage, spirit and integrity of American women everywhere."

So began on October 7, 1940, on CBS radio what was to become one of America's most beloved and long running **soap operas** (1939) — melodramas most often underwritten by manufacturers of laundry soap.

Truly a washday miracle — emotions, like grime, coming out in the wash. Unfortunately, genuine **passion** fares not quite as well.

In early Christian times, **passion** referred to the "suffering" at its roots. By the end of the 14th century, it signified powerful emotions such as anger and tender ones such as love. It's since been reduced to the violent stirrings of sexual love.

Sympathy, composed of the Greek *sym*, "with" and *pathos*, "suffering" or "feeling," should leave us sharing in the feelings or joined in the suffering of other human beings. The Spanish are **sympatico**, but we only care enough to send our very best.

All "pretty **pathetic**," you say. In 1598, **pathetic** meant "moving" or "stirring." By 1737, it began arousing "pity." Now it's simply "woeful." So with **soap operas** and TV fare in general — **bathetic** (c.1834) from the Greek word for "depth," speaking directly to their shallowness.

What better occasion than Valentine's day to make sure **your heart's in the right place** — insuring that you're intentions are truly honorable.

Heart in your mouth? Uh-uh. There's where you get that choking feeling from fear, guilt, or shyness, the heart beating so fast and furiously, it feels as if it were jumping upward.

On your sleeve? Not there either. It was proper back in more chivalric times for knights to pin milady's favor to their sleeve. It's now considered gauche to show unrequited love quite so publicly.

But don't keep your feelings locked inside either. Come right out and say them **straight from the heart**, wherever it may be.

Expressing your feelings is the surest way to **warm the cockles** of that special someone's heart. Remember Mary, the contrary one of nursery rhyme fame, who counted **cockleshells** among her favorite flowers? The **cockleshell** after which the flower was named is merely the valve of the **cockle**, a palatable mollusk, the shape of which 17th century anatomists compared to the ventricle of the heart. Others took to the analogy, and they've occupied a warm spot for us ever since.

On this day of all days, it's no time to clam up, and that's **from the heart**.

Words sure travel a funny path, as do the intentions which drive them. Take **charity** for example.

An old Biblical favorite, it originally referred to Christian love, between man and God, and man and neighbor. "**Charity began at home**" during the early 14th century, as did its darker variation, "**Charity and beating begin at home**."

With its institutionalization, we began to hear "**cold as charity**," a stark reversal of the original intent of the word. This spoke directly to what the **charitable** act felt like to the recipients from their prolonged dealings with **charitable** institutions, the only way available to them to express their feelings of wounded self-respect and their accompanying loss of dignity. Today the word has become so compromised that the recipients themselves totally reject what was once our most universal expression of love and care. "Don't want any **charity**," they say.

Ditto for **welfare**. **Wel fare** first meant a "good journey" or "safe arrival," later "prosperity" and even "merrymaking." Today's **welfare recipients** have had anything but a smooth journey and in no sense, can be said to have "arrived." The popular perception, however, is that of prolonged partying. Like **charity**, **welfare** has also lost its way.

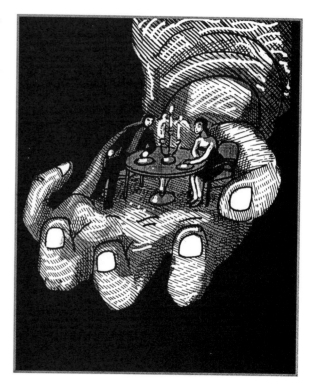

Time for a **heart to heart talk** with our politicians.

The heart is cognate with the Latin *cor* and the Greek *Kardia*. Because of its position and importance in the body, it became the center or **core** of things, as in the **heart of the matter**. It also gave us **cardiac** arrest and made us **cordial**, "warm and friendly" — the civility so sadly lacking in contemporary life, as well as naming a **hearty** drink.

But what would life be without a little **heartache**? During the Middle Ages the **Order of the Bleeding Heart** honored the Virgin Mary "whose heart was pierced by many sorrows."

They didn't touch Westbrook Pegler however. The noted conservative columnist of the 30s and 40s derisively labeled those calling for governmental intervention in rectifying social ills, as "**bleeding heart liberals**."

Such **bleeding hearts** appear now stilled. New programs from Congress to feed the hungry? **Eat your heart out**. Something For the homeless? How about a **heart as big as all outdoors**. That's where you'll find them.

A plea to those in power: please **take heart**. Somehow, find the **courage** to act on the basis of principle, rather than expediency.

The very sound of the word is depressing. Can you imagine a candidate running for office with that name? **Dole.**

It's a word associated with bums, breadlines, and incompetents — from the Old English *daelan*, to "divide, distribute, or share out," from *dael* a "part," e.g. your lot in life, "getting what has been **dealt** out to you."

Mix in some *dolor*, Latin for "grief," and *dolore*, to "grieve or be in pain," and it can only make you **doleful**, as in "grief," "sadness," or "lament."

Nowadays, you'll find just about everyone's on the **dole,** from corporate America to motorists.

What causes us most grief, however, is the Poor. So we **dole** out to them only limited and carefully measured amounts, often so meager as to cause us to add our **condolences**.

However, for those deemed **indolent** — literally, "those who do not grieve," we have nothing but contempt, treating them the same as criminals who fail to show remorse.

The poor person failing to grieve is obviously without pain, making his condition a function of his own sloth, thus rendering him undeserving of our attention and support. Could anything be more **doleful**?

How do we gauge the health of a nation? Most look to its economic indicators — how **wealthy** it is. Closer examination reveals, however, that they might have confused "health" with "**wealth**."

That's understandable. **Wealth** (*weal*) first conveyed "wellness," a general sense of happiness. Only later did it evolve into "abundance," as in "a **wealth** of personal talent." Not until the 18th century did it become associated with money and possessions, flowering fully with the fruition of capitalism. Today, all general references to happiness and well being have been dropped from the word. Money is what it's all about.

We also once knew the word *commonweal,* "a general sense of well-being of the total **community**."

T.S. Eliot asked. "What is the meaning of this city? Do you huddle close together because you love one another? What will you answer? 'We all dwell together to make money from each other'? or 'This is a **community**'?"

The Latin *munia,* "services." left some **immune**, *im,* "not" having to be inconvenienced by doing public service. It also created **community** from *com,* "with", "those bound together in service" to one another. In this lies the true **wealth** of a nation.

CHAPTER 11

Blame

WHODUNNIT

WHY ALWAYS ME DOC?

SCAPEGOAT MEETS WITH SHRINK…

Looking for someone to blame?

Among all creatures large and small, you can't beat the goat, an animal long associated through myth with evil.

His story begins in the Old Testament where on the day of atonement two goats were chosen, one to be offered as a pure sacrifice to the Lord, the other to be sent alive into the wilderness and on whose head was symbolically laid the sins of the people. In the Revised version the freed goat was given the Hebrew name *Azazel with* the word "dismissal" written in the margin.

In 1530, while translating the Bible, the Reverend William Tyndale substituted the word "scape," meaning "escape" to describe the freed creature, creating the world's first **scapegoat**.

Tyndale hoped his translation would make the Bible more widely available. Unfortunately, the Church thought otherwise. They burnt his books and put him to death at the stake, making him into a latter day **scapegoat**.

Find this all somewhat **capricious**? Indeed! From the Latin *caprum,* "belonging to a goat." You know how those goats are — neither polite nor predictable. Not very big on etiquette either.

All Day Suckers

Wherever you go, you'll find a **sucker**. But don't blame him on P.T. Barnum. Though often attributed to him, he never said, "there's one born every minute."

The **sucker's** self sufficient, getting around quite well on his own. Thank you. Linguistically, he's played many a role — everything from a "parasite," "sponger," and "greenhorn," to a "simpleton" — even a "babe," from his primary vocation.

Some, however, prefer the **whipping boy** — from a 17th century British custom whereby punishment merited by a young prince or royal personage was transferred to another youth. William Murray was the first **whipping boy**, receiving floggings for the son of James I, later Charles I.

Still looking for a **patsy**? He's been standard American slang for the classic victim or dupe since 1910. Among his possible derivations are *Pasqualino,* the diminutive for *Pasquale,* who in Italian described "a particularly vulnerable man or boy."

You also might find his roots in *Pasqua,* "Easter," and the Pascal sacrifice of an innocent lamb. Or *pazzo,* "fool," from the Pazzi family of 15th century Florence who were foolish enough to challenge the power of the Medicis.

Gee! The lengths people will go to find a **patsy**.

IN PASSING...

We've been **passing the buck** since the first settlers received deerskins in barter with the Native Americans. Though the skins of both the male and female deer were traded, it was the skin of the male deer, the **buck**, that was more highly valued.

Between 1700 and 1750, a quarter to half a million buckskins were traded annually on the American frontier. By 1720 they had become a unit of exchange and a measure of wealth, and people were calling them **bucks**. About 1856 they became identified with our most popular currency, the dollar.

How did we come to **pass the buck**? Card players used to keep a marker in front of them to serve as a reminder as to whose deal it was. The marker used was frequently a silver dollar, hence the reference to it as the **buck** — **passing** from player to player each time the deal changed. The expression, **passing the buck** then became synonymous with placing responsibility elsewhere.

Don't really care? "Just bag it," you say.

Uh-uh. As Harry Truman reminded us, "the **buck** stops here."

An early Latin proverb noted how "dogs do not eat fellow dogs." Since 1732, however, it's been a **dog-eat-dog world**. A world where you have to know how **to do a number on someone** — "how to humiliate an adversary totally."

When **doing a number** on the stage, you simply "performed your assigned role." **Doing a number on someone** (1960s-70s) meant you incorporated him into your act, putting him totally at your mercy.

This often entailed giving him **the short end of the stick**, from the ritual of breaking the wishbone of a cooked bird — the person with the long end getting his wish, or from the drawing of straws to determine who would do an unpleasant or dangerous task.

There are those, however, who prefer **throwing** whoever is bugging them **to the wolves** (early 20thC.). When being pursued by predators, it's an effective ploy to throw them something to chew on in order to divert their attention from yourself. Who better than an insufferable colleague or subordinate?

There's always the risk of **crying wolf** (late 17thC.), "giving a false alarm" — from the fable of the shepherd lad who lost credibility for doing it so often, that when a real wolf appeared, no one came to his assistance. A ploy less than a howling success.

Departing slightly from the fowl mood of the book, we would make one last effort to make things **ducky**.

Lord love a duck!... "Good heavens" (1917). Look, at the ease with which he **takes to water** and how troubles just **roll off his back**.

In the early 19th century, he was **a duck of a fellow**, "a lovely or fine example," and when **ducky**, a real "sweetheart **.**"

But as easily as he **ducks** into water, we've been **ducking** (late19th C.) to get away from someone, keeping out of sight by **copping** or **doing a duck** (c.1889), or by just **ducking out** — thus "evading responsibility."

We finally became responsible during the 1970s, by **having all our ducks in a row, lining them up** — "arranging our affairs in a business-like manner." Unfortunately, **sitting ducks** have long been an easy target, individually or **all in a row**, increasing the likelihood of their ending up as **duck soup** (c.1902). This makes it a "breeze," an "easily accomplished task," thanks to T.A. Dorgan, the noted cartoonist and wordsmith.

Have we been **playing ducks and drakes** (19th C.) all along — just "wasting your time foolishly?" **Can a duck swim?** "Emphatically yes" (c.1892).

Ropes of sand (17thC.) are "ineffective" or "futile ties" which lack both permanence and binding power. But when you're **on the ropes,** you're "at the brink of collapse," or "on the verge of defeat." Like a boxer whose back is up against them, your only option is to swing back wildly

There are those who know how to turn the situation to their own advantage, like Mohammed Ali and his famed **rope-a-dope.** Like a rigger on a 19th century clipper ship, he **knew the ropes** — "had a fully detailed understanding of what he was doing."

A ship's ropes composed a complex system of lines which controlled the sails. **Knowing the ropes** meant you understood how to operate them properly. That failing, you might find yourself **at the end of your rope,** "at the limit of your resources, abilities, or endurance," putting you in a situation similar to a tied up animal whose tether restricts its movement.

If you haven't figured it out by now, this can only spell the **bitter end.** The **bitt** or **bitter** of a ship was a timber crosspiece or other strong piece of wood or iron projecting above deck for securing lines, cables, and chains belayed around it. When you reached **the bitter end,** you were literally **at the end of your rope.**

Hang in there gang!

Index